PRESSURE GROUP

PRESSURE GROUP

The Campaign for
Commercial Television

by H. H. WILSON

London
SECKER & WARBURG

PRINTED IN GREAT BRITAIN BY
C. TINLING & CO. LIMITED,
LIVERPOOL, LONDON AND PRESCOT
AND FIRST PUBLISHED 1961 BY
MARTIN SECKER & WARBURG LTD.,
14 CARLISLE STREET, LONDON, W.C.1

To
ROBERT S. LYND
friend, scholar, teacher

CONTENTS

CORRIGENDUM

P. 96, line 25. The secretary of the
Conservative Parliamentary Broadcasting
Committee was not Mr Chapman-
Walker but Mr Peter Goldman.

CORRIGENDUM

The Author and the Publishers wish to correct any implication that Mr. C. I. Orr-Ewing, M.P., had any personal financial interest in the initiation of Commercial T.V., and accept Mr. Orr-Ewing's statement that, during his association with the Company, Messrs. A. C. Cossor Ltd were never concerned as to how T.V. programmes were organised or created, and took no financial interest in any commercial T.V. company.

They also accept Mr. Orr-Ewing's assurance that it is not the case that he ever formed or joined any unofficial group as stated on pages 63 and 69. Mr. Orr-Ewing has informed them that he served on the official Conservative Broadcasting Committee, and was also a member, on the invitation of the Conservative Chief Whip, of the Ralph Assheton Committee which was specially set up in February 1951.

PREFACE

THIS IS AN attempt to describe what was in essence an intraparty conflict over the introduction and passage of a single piece of legislation, the Independent Television Act. Apart from the intrinsic interest in the change in the position of a venerated institution, the British Broadcasting Corporation, it is intended to provide some insight into the actual operation of the Conservative Parliamentary Party and its relation to external pressures. Though it has become a commonplace to speak of the Member of Parliament as powerless to oppose the authority and prestige of the Cabinet, it was hoped that detailed analysis of a single "revolt" might suggest circumstances in which individual Conservative Members can successfully influence events.

Most studies of pressure groups are able to rely on published documents, annual reports and trade journals. Because of the peculiar nature of this particular Parliamentary conflict it was essential, and unavoidable, to reconstruct its development by means of interviews with individuals who had been directly concerned with one or another phase of these events. Admittedly a difficult and even hazardous method, it is often the only way the student may be able to produce a realistic account. Few individuals or organizations had complete records even of their own participation, and none had knowledge of all phases. Some were reluctant to permit scrutiny of existing files, many were too preoccupied with current interests to afford time for interviews. There are obvious hazards in attempting to recreate even so minor an historical episode—men are busy, memories are short, and public men are sometimes understandably reluctant to record details of political controversy. One comes away from such a study as this with admiration, if not downright awe, for historians who write with confidence about men and events long past. Starting to pick up the threads just four years after the resolution of this issue, one found that documents were dispersed and incomplete, that several principals were in other continents, and still others were already dead.

Despite these obstacles every effort was made to verify details. Intensive use was made of newspaper and periodical files to establish a chronology of events, *Hansard* was studied intensively for clues and interpretations, interviews were cross-checked and verified to the extent possible. Ultimately, of course, where there are conflicting versions and differing interpretations the author must himself decide. Since in many instances individuals requested that they should not be quoted, some statements must rest solely on the authority of the author.

I am indebted to the following individuals for their courtesy and generosity in granting interviews, which in several instances were expanded and clarified by correspondence: Members of Parliament, Lord Morrison of Lambeth, Sir Leslie Plummer, Anthony Wedgwood Benn, Christopher Mayhew, Patrick Gordon Walker, Lord Simon of Wythenshawe, Lord Shackleton, Enoch Powell, Captain L. P. S. Orr, Charles Orr-Ewing, John Rodgers, A. E. Cooper, Sir Beverley Baxter, Martin Madden, Lord Woolton, Lady Gammans, and Lord Boothby. Representatives of advertising: Drummond Armstrong, Colman, Prentis & Varley, Ltd.; A. N. C. Varley, Colman, Prentis & Varley, Ltd.; R. A. Benson, S. H. Benson, Ltd.; Dan Ingman, Young & Rubicam; Cyrus Ducker, Dolan, Ducker, Whitcomb & Stewart, Ltd.; James O'Connor, Institute of Practitioners in

Advertising; Michael Patmore, J. Walter Thompson Co. Ltd.; J. R. M. Brumwell, The Advertising Services Guild; John Metcalf, John Hobson & Partners, Ltd.; and James Archibald, J. Walter Thompson Co., Ltd. From the Conservative Political Centre and Popular Television Association: Peter Goldman, Mark Chapman-Walker, Ronald Simms, and Gordon McIvor. Others included: Mrs. Mary Stocks, Beveridge Committee; A. W. Pragnell, Independent Television Authority; Professor A. J. P. Taylor; Sir Ben Barnett, Post Office; Sir William Haley, *The Times*; Sir Ian Jacob and Harman Grisewood of the BBC; Norman Collins, Associated Television Ltd.; Kenneth Winckles, the Rank Organization; Lord Bessborough, Benson Lonsdale & Co.; W. A. Twyman, TV Audience Measurement, Ltd.; Eric Croston, Public Relations Editor, Associated Television, Ltd.; S. E. Allchurch, Radio Industry Council; and Maurice Winnick, Popular Television Association. Lady Violet Bonham-Carter and Mr. L. E. Room, Director-General of The Advertising Association, provided helpful information by correspondence.

I wish also to express my gratitude to those in the Conservative Party, the radio-television industry, advertising and trade associations who were most helpful but for personal or professional reasons requested that their names be withheld.

To the BBC's Librarian and his staff I am indebted for every kindness and assistance in making use of that excellent library.

Generous friends and colleagues criticized the manuscript at various stages. I am particularly indebted to Burton Paulu, Arnold Rogow, H. R. G. Greaves, Harvey Glickman, Graeme Moodie, Robert Engler, Paul Tillett and Donald Riddle.

To Cora Kaye Wilson I am indebted for sensitive criticism, confident certainty that the task would be completed, and quiet encouragement.

INTRODUCTION

On July 30, 1954, the bill creating the Independent Television Authority became law, thereby ending the monopoly of broadcasting which the British Broadcasting Corporation had sustained for twenty-seven years. The first commercial broadcast from the London station of the new Authority went on the air fourteen months later, September 22, 1955, and by 1961 some ninety-five per cent of the population was within reach of the ITA operating stations.

Unquestionably the passage of the Television Act is one of the most interesting and significant political actions of the post-war period. Not only did it arouse a most bitter and prolonged political debate, but it marked a decisive change in what had been considered a peculiarly British social invention, the BBC. Its importance goes far beyond any question of the merits of commercial versus public service broadcasting, for to many it seems to symbolize a change within the Conservative Party and gives expression to an accumulation of influences which are shaping the future of British society.

This is a political study, an attempt to present the history of the events, forces, techniques involved in the passage of a single controversial legislative act. It is an effort to reconstruct the course of events leading to a quite drastic institutional change. The focus of the study is on the political and, to a lesser extent, on the social factors involved. It does not attempt to evaluate the merits of the change in the pattern of British broadcasting, beyond presenting the arguments of advocates and opponents of the innovation.[1] Though there is no problem of party political partisanship in treating this subject, there are two biases against which readers may be forewarned. First is a general scepticism of the desirability of permitting any medium of communication to be dominated by a single control, no matter how enlightened and responsible it may be; and second, is a doubt that so vital an instrument as television should be utilized for commercial purposes.

Caution certainly dictates restraint in generalizing on the basis of a single legislative enactment. Yet as an example of a successful pressure group operation, the passage of the Television Act warrants analysis, even though it be pressure politics with differences not readily to be subsumed under the usual descriptions.[2] Two special, one-purpose organizations were created, the National Television Council to oppose commercial broadcasting, and the Popular Television Association to promote it. The permanent, formal trade associations, the normal instruments of pressure politics, that were most directly concerned—advertising bodies and radio-television manufacturers—proclaimed an official policy of neutrality that was, perhaps, more apparent than real.

Its interest as a case study may even be enhanced by its deviation from more orthodox pressure politics, especially if it be true that it reveals political techniques that continue to be used by one of the major parties. For an observer a most curious aspect of the history of this Act is the defeat of the Conservative Party leadership by a very small group of nominally politically insignificant Conservative backbenchers. Actually, of course, they were not insignificant because they were, in effect, spokesmen for powerful economic groups in the Conservative coalition, e.g. the radio-television manufacturing industry, major American and British advertising agencies, and financial institutions. Furthermore, they were re-inforced by the professional publicity and public relations practitioners who had been brought into the Conservative

Central Office by Lord Woolton when he reorganized the Party after July 1, 1946.

This is conceived as a case study of the actual operation of power *within* the Conservative coalition, an example of behind the scenes manoeuvring to force a significant decision. How was a reluctant Party leadership persuaded to go along with this innovation? There seems to be evidence that Sir Winston Churchill, Lord Salisbury, Sir Anthony Eden, Mr. R. A. Butler and others of the Conservative Cabinet were far from enthusiastic about introducing commercial television, even though they may have had theoretical reservations about the BBC as a monopoly. Other Conservative leaders—Lord Halifax, Lord Waverley, Lord Brand—were actively and vehemently opposed to this action, as was so enthusiastic a Tory politician as Lord Hailsham. In actuality there seems initially to have been no significant Party leadership support for commercial television, except for Lord Woolton, whose role was somewhat ambiguous.

Why should the Party which created the BBC and originally established its monopoly control over broadcasting now turn against it, introducing a pattern which must undermine, or at least modify, the original conception of broadcasting as a public service? Why was this change instituted at a time when the Corporation's prestige was never greater? Perhaps no other institution had so completely and peculiarly represented the British way of life and the British genius for institutional innovation than had the BBC. To foreigners, especially during and after World War II, the BBC symbolized the best in British political democracy. Yet within two years of taking power in 1951, the Conservative Government had endorsed commercial television, an action thought by many Conservatives to be antithetic to the perpetuation of traditional philosophic conservatism and a concession to the opportunistic, or practical, Conservatism. The action was certainly a defeat for what has been loosely characterized as "The Establishment", a fact illustrated by the distinguished status of the opponents. This would, in itself, suggest a change in the orientation of the Conservative Party, as well as suggesting the direction of movement within British society. It is likely that the proponents of commercial television were more closely in tune with large segments of the populace, particularly Labour voters, than were the defenders of the BBC. The public, however, played no part in the decision; though undoubtedly those who owned sets favoured having an additional channel, there was no public demand for the introduction of a commercial system.

One may conclude that the introduction of commercial television must inevitably speed the commercialization of society, a fact noted by several of the opponents. Ironically, this innovation seemed to many a long step in the direction of "Americanization" of British society, and it was taken by the Party representing those who had been most vehement in condemning American (i.e. vulgar) influence. Thus the Conservative Party sanctioned a development which, its critics maintained, speeds the movement towards a society which would glorify middle class consumption goals and the commercialization of all institutional and personal relationships and values. For the introduction of commercial television needs to be viewed in conjunction with other policies of the practical Conservatives who were inspired by Lord Woolton to crusade against the Labour Government's declared intent to make operative a social ethic. His programme was conceived and ideally designed to associate "Tory democracy" with the consumption aspirations of the majority. Many of its advocates were perceptive enough to understand that the subtle and long-term impact of commercial television would re-inforce the political results of the vast expansion of hire-purchase, government subsidized loans for home ownership, the drive to get low income groups to purchase shares of corporate stocks, and the pervasive growth of advertising inspired by motivational research. They had observed and benefited from American experience in selling "people's capitalism" in a welfare state.[3] With other media, commercial television operates to "interlace the consumption expectations of their readers and listeners with the interests of their backers and advertisers. . . . The rise of the consumption-oriented individual of mass society thus sets the stage for the shrinkage of the ideologically oriented nineteenth-century party."[4]

CHAPTER I

THE BRITISH BROADCASTING
CORPORATION

BROADCASTING IN BRITAIN began as a commercial enterprise when, in the interest of increasing the sale of radio receivers, six radio equipment manufacturers provided the original capital to form the British Broadcasting Company in December, 1922.[1] Direct advertising was banned from the beginning, though sponsors might finance programmes in exchange for having their names mentioned. Revenue for the Company came from royalties on the sale of sets, half the ten-shilling licence fee collected by the Post Office, and the original stock subscription. From the start broadcasting was, in practice, a monopoly, although the Postmaster-General always had the authority to licence other agencies.

Financial difficulties of the Company led the Postmaster-General in 1923 to appoint a committee under the chairmanship of Major-General Sir Frederick Sykes, and composed of representatives from the Press, radio industry, Parliament and the Post Office. The immediate result of the Sykes Report on future developments was the extension of the Company's licence to December 31, 1926. But the Committee had suggested that because of its social and political possibilities, "the control of such a potential power over public opinion and the life of the nation ought to remain with the state, and that the operation of so important a national service ought not to be allowed to become an unrestricted commercial monopoly."[2] The Committee did not recommend that there should be a public monopoly, but only that public control over broadcasting was essential. In fact, it recommended that "subject to existing rights, the Government should keep its hands free to grant additional licences, and should consider various alternatives for the operation in the future, either by the Company or by other authorities, of local or relay stations in addition to large stations."[3]

Following a further investigation by the Crawford Committee in 1926, the British Broadcasting Corporation was established as a public corporation in January, 1927. This first Charter and Licence (1927-1936) established the principles that have governed the Corporation, with minor modifications, ever since. Financed by licence fees on households equipped with radio sets, in practice a monopoly, though legally the Postmaster-General could always have issued other licences, the BBC was to be independent of the Government in its day-to-day operations, despite the fact that ultimate control remained with the state. The government's ultimate control was in principle absolute; it included the right to require the BBC to broadcast government material on request, the right to veto material, general or particular, to control the hours of broadcasting, to appoint and dismiss Governors, and to allocate finances. Nevertheless, the independence which the Crawford Committee recommended was established, and in practice it has been the policy of all governments to respect the operating independence of the Corporation. Though individual Members of Parliament might ask questions of the Postmaster-General on broad policy matters, this potential interference has been limited by the authority of the Minister to refuse to discuss subjects involving day-to-day operations.

There have been three additional Charters granted, and two additional committees of inquiry, Lord Ullswater's

Committee of 1935 and Lord Beveridge's Committee in 1949.[4] Though the committees submitted criticisms of some aspects of the Corporation's practice, all recommended a continuation of the general pattern and purpose of the BBC.

For the future of British broadcasting, the most important action taken by the original Company was its appointment of Mr. J. C. W. Reith as General Manager.* With the formation of the public corporation he became its first Director-General, remaining with the BBC until 1938. Professor Coase has concluded that it was Reith's influence which established the belief that unified control of broadcasting was essential for its most effective development. Though technical and administrative considerations were a factor, both for Reith and the Post Office, there is no doubt that unified control was desired by Reith to maintain standards. By the time the Crawford Committee met "there appears to have been general support among those who wrote or spoke about broadcasting both that broadcasting should in Great Britain remain a monopoly and that it should in future be directed by a Board representing interests wider than those of the radio trade."[5] Reith conceived of broadcasting as a public service which must maintain definite standards and be guided by moral responsibility, both intellectual and ethical. Its primary function was to provide information and education and not merely to entertain. The service should, he felt, bring into a maximum number of homes the best in every department of human knowledge, endeavour and achievement. To this end, Reith viewed a monopoly by the BBC as imperative. Before the Beveridge Committee in 1950, Reith restated his conviction that "it was the brute force of monopoly that enabled the BBC to become what it did; and to do what it did; that made it possible for a policy of moral responsibility to be followed."[6] There is general agreement

* He became Sir John Reith in 1927, and Lord Reith in 1940.

that he more than any other person shaped the development and provided the philosophy that has guided the BBC from its inception. "Historically speaking," wrote Charles A. Siepmann in 1950, "it is the personality of one man that accounts for broadcasting in Britain as it is today. Sir John Reith was so certain he was right that no research seemed necessary. Regardless of its actual effects, for him his policy stood self-justified. Secure in his personal conviction of what was right and wrong, he imposed upon a nation the imprint of his personality."[7]

Throughout the Reith administration the BBC was able, because of frequency shortages, to provide only two networks. There was a uniform National Service and a Regional Service which broadcast local programmes. Though not entirely ignoring popular taste, the philosophy of giving the public "something slightly better than it now thinks it likes" and the fact that until 1939 there was no systematic study of audience reaction, made for a limited choice and somewhat inflexible programming. The "Reith Sunday" with its fare restricted to religious talks and serious music became notorious.

World War II drastically altered the BBC and Lord Reith's conception of broadcasting. All radio was consolidated into one national network, the Home Service, and the pioneering television experiments, which since 1936 had given Britain the world's first regular television programme, were closed down. Six months after the BBC had gone on a war footing, a second national service was introduced as the General Forces Programme, which was made available in Britain and to British Forces throughout the world. This network and the American Forces Network which was developed to meet the needs of American troops stationed in Britain, naturally featured entertainment. As a result, more Britishers were introduced to programmes (minus commercials) and broadcasters from Canada and the United States. There is little doubt that British soldiers and civilians alike thoroughly enjoyed the more relaxed, informal atmosphere of American-style broadcasting and found the entertainment more sprightly than that of the pre-war BBC. To some extent, at least, the dreaded "Americanization" of British tastes by Hollywood and "pop" records was given additional impetus by the American Forces Network.

Under wartime conditions it was also inevitable that the Government would be much more immediately concerned with broadcasting than had previously been the case. The Ministry of Information exerted general supervision, assuming certain of the powers exercised in peacetime by the Postmaster-General, but the BBC continued to be responsible for the selection of subject matter and regarded the news as inviolate. In addition, both domestic and foreign services were financed by direct parliamentary grants-in-aid. There was a tremendous expansion of the Overseas Services as the BBC came to be the only reliable news source and the voice of Britain for people throughout the world, and especially in German-occupied Europe. This wartime development, in which a broadcasting monopoly seemed to be virtually an arm of the state, may have contributed to the genuine concern of those who in 1946 pressed for a re-examination of the Corporation's role.[8]

After the War, under Sir William Haley who became Director-General in 1944, the wartime programme development was continued, although the full independence of the BBC from Government departments was quickly re-established by the Labour Government. The Home Service with the restored regional variations again became the balanced core of BBC service; the General Forces Programme, with some efforts to raise listeners' standards, became the Light Programme; and, in September, 1946, the completely unique Third Programme went on the air.

Deliberately designed to appeal to the serious listener, the Third Programme ignored radio's subservience to segmented time or the dictates of the mass audience. "It aims to broadcast, without regard to length or difficulty, the masterpieces of music, art, and letters which lend themselves to transmission in sound."[9] Handicapped by wave-length difficulties, the Third was available to only about 55 per cent of the population until 1950, when it could be received by about 70 per cent. Widely admired by many foreigners and a matter of pride to those in England who were concerned that minority interests and the intelligentsia should not be ignored by a public service, the Third Programme concept was always subjected to criticism by some as an extravagant use of limited wave-lengths. Such criticism did not come only from those who were hungry for commercial outlets and contemptuous of BBC concern for cultural and intellectual standards. Lord Reith, for one, considered the Third Programme objectionable as "a waste of a precious wavelength." "Much of its matter is too limited in appeal; the rest should have a wider audience," he told the Beveridge Committee. "Its existence is taken to condone the absence of policy elsewhere; it is an easy way out."[10] Whatever their views on the Third Programme, most listeners were likely to agree that the post-war BBC was offering far more attractive fare than ever before. It had come a long way in meeting the needs of the British public, without deviating from its public service mission.

From the beginning the BBC always faced at least limited competition. In 1924 radio relay exchanges, or wire broadcasting, began to develop throughout the country. The relay companies provided programmes which were sent over wires to a loudspeaker in the home of a subscriber. The service had the attraction of having quite modest weekly charges, including repair service, and providing a limited selection of programmes with interference-free reception. By 1950 there were over three hundred of these exchanges licensed by the Post Office with approximately one million subscribers. There might well have been many more had not half the county boroughs refused permission to install the transmission wires.[11]

These exchanges were distributors of programmes, not producers. Prior to the Ullswater Report, the relay exchanges were free to take whatever BBC programmes they wanted and to include an unlimited amount of commercially sponsored programmes from the Continent, so that subscribers actually had access to more stations than could be received by most sets. Inevitably the exchanges were opposed by the BBC because they could distort the balanced programme approach of the Corporation. This hostility was shared by the newspapers who feared that the foreign commercial programmes might siphon off advertising revenue, and by the radio manufacturing industry because subscribers to the service did not have to buy receiving sets. Although the Ullswater Committee recommendation that the relay exchanges be owned and operated by the Post Office and the programmes be controlled by the BBC was not acted upon, after 1937 more stringent controls were applied. The exchanges were not permitted to originate any programmes; no political, social or religious propaganda in English was to be relayed from a foreign station; with two programmes offered to subscribers, one must be BBC in origin and the second must carry BBC programmes at least seventy-five per cent of the time; if three channels were offered, two must always be BBC; and no money was to be taken by the exchange company for relaying a programme.

More serious competition for the BBC was provided by Continental stations, primarily Radio Luxembourg and Radio Normandy, broadcasting in English and beaming programmes to the United Kingdom. The International Broadcasting Company was founded in 1930 by Captain Leonard F. Plugge to transmit commercial programmes from Radio Normandy. The Luxembourg station, the more important of the two, began broadcasting commercial programmes to Britain in 1933. With the BBC week-day schedule starting at

10.15 a.m. and the "Reith Sunday" limited to serious and religious programmes, Radio Luxembourg acquired a substantial audience, variously estimated at four million to six million listeners. Radio Normandy was estimated to have had in 1938 an "average audience of 1,229,000."[12] By 1938 a number of large British firms, chiefly producers of cosmetics, drugs and foods, were spending over £1,500,000 "on sponsored programmes to England from foreign countries."[13] Thanks largely to the attractiveness of the post-war Light Programme it is likely that Radio Luxembourg did not attract so numerous an audience when it resumed broadcasting after the war.* However, it continued to attract British advertisers who sponsored programmes featuring popular music, some light drama, and a number of American religious revivalists.

The BBC always opposed these commercial broadcasts from the Continent on the grounds that they undermined the programme standards of the public service and because Radio Luxembourg operated on a wave-length not assigned to it by international agreement. All British governments agreed with this attitude and tried by diplomatic negotiation, currency regulations, and agreements at the International Wavelength Conferences to discourage such commercial broadcasting. Through the Post Office the foreign-based station was denied the use of telephone lines to relay broadcasts from London, so many programmes were recorded in England and flown to Luxembourg. To safeguard against the political use of foreign stations, Parliament, in the Representation of the People Act, 1949, specifically prohibited their use by any candidate during an election.

The existence of the relay exchanges and the Continental stations meant that several million British people were experiencing commercial broadcasting and not only had no objection to the advertising, but preferred the programmes

* Radio Normandy did not resume broadcasting to England after the war.

to those offered by the BBC.* The many British firms who advertised through these media became convinced that radio was an effective marketing instrument and therefore determined to obtain full access to the medium in Britain. In these ways the relay exchanges and the Continental stations played a significant part in determining the future of the BBC and the conception of public service broadcasting.

* *The Advertisers' Weekly*, April 7, 1949, reported a survey conducted for Radio Luxembourg Advertising, Ltd., by the British Market Research Bureau, which indicated that about 24 per cent of households in Britain listened to Radio Luxembourg, and that only 3 out of 2,500 housewives mentioned that programmes were "spoilt by advertising" or that they "didn't bother about commercial or advertising programmes."

CHAPTER II

THE CONCERN WITH MONOPOLY

WITH THE 1936 BBC Charter due to expire at the end of 1946, it was not surprising that there should have been an increasing volume of questions concerning the Corporation's future. By and large, those asking questions in the House of Commons represented all parties and appeared not to have been primarily advocates of commercial broadcasting. There is evidence that need for additional revenue was influencing some of the Members to look for other sources of income, especially to sustain the more costly television. Even Members who favoured commercial broadcasting seem to have been primarily motivated by doubts about the monopoly aspect of the BBC.

On January 29, 1946, Mr. Barnett Janner (Labour) asked that an inquiry be made before the licence fee was raised. He urged on the Government a review of BBC activities "to examine to what extent its present programmes meet public requirements and what other sources of possible revenue exist in addition to licence receipts. . . ." Mr. Herbert Morrison, Lord President of the Council, replied that the Government had decided to increase the licence fee after full consideration, that "other issues" were under consideration, and that the Prime Minister, Mr. Attlee, did not think it necessary to have a special inquiry.[1] A Ministerial Committee under the chairmanship of Mr. Arthur Greenwood, Lord Privy Seal, had decided that no inquiry was

essential before renewing the Charter. In Febr
Prime Minister, replying to Mr. Janner and to
Crookshank, who had also requested an inquiry, 1
the Government's decision that no investigat   ..~
necessary and emphasized that the previous Coalition
Government had decided against an independent inquiry.[2]

There was widespread criticism of the Labour Government's decision. Throughout the spring, questions were
raised by Members, and a great deal of resentment was
reported within the Labour Party at the Government's
refusal. Welsh Members were said to be especially dissatisfied since they felt that Wales did not receive fair
treatment from the BBC. It is perhaps symptomatic of
considerable Labour rank-and-file dissatisfaction with the
BBC that a motion before the Scottish Trade Union Congress
in April should have called for replacing the BBC Charter
with an Act of Parliament which would place responsibility
in the hands of a Minister; developing regional services;
establishing advisory committees in each area to represent
political parties, unions and cultural societies; and freedom
of speech "as a matter of right," with political parties being
given broadcast time each month.[3] And in the course of an
adjournment debate it became obvious that members of all
parties from Wales and Scotland were demanding the establishment of independent broadcasting corporations in their
countries and, to this end, favoured an independent inquiry.[4]

Though there was sporadic criticism of BBC programmes,
there seemed to have been two significant factors operating
to strengthen the conviction that an inquiry was desirable.
Many individuals felt that during the war the BBC had lost
much of its previous independence and had become virtually
the instrument of the Government.* This was accepted as

* For example, see Sir Ian Fraser's statement, June 11, 1952:
H. C. Debs. 502:264-265.
Some six to eight months before the war, according to Fraser, "It
was proposed by the Ministers who were preparing for defence that

inevitable, even desirable, in wartime but was distrusted as a serious threat to political freedom in peacetime. As expressed by *The Times*, the war had tended to break down Lord Reith's principles without setting others in their place and the recent weakness of the BBC was due to its trying to do too many things and serve too many requirements.[5] Secondly, many Conservatives were still suffering from the shock produced by their electoral defeat in 1945, a traumatic experience which some Conservatives felt the BBC had intensified with "a pro-Labour bias". Their fears of permanent tenure in the political wilderness were enhanced by an addiction to their own propaganda which convinced them that the Labour Party intended a genuine social revolution in which the BBC would become a powerful force operating to perpetuate Socialist rule.* Mr. Churchill was especially fearful of the Labour Government's intentions, spurred on as it was by what he considered to be the social revolutionary tendencies of Labour backbenchers. The absence of any evidence to sustain such a fantasy did not mitigate Conservative devotion to it; it was a phenomenon to be understood not in the light of what is known now, but rather in the Conservative mood of 1945.

---

directly war came the BBC Board of Governors should be abolished and a dictatorship, composed of the Director-General and his assistant, should be established under the orders of some Minister connected with the war organization." Dr. Mallon, a fellow Governor and Labour Party member, joined with Fraser in protesting the change. "We did succeed in retaining the rudiments of a Board by our own struggles inside the Corporation. Instead of having a Director-General we maintained a Board consisting of two persons instead of the proper number, but within a year or so matters changed and the Board was re-established."

* A view expressed editorially in *The Scotsman*, Edinburgh, when commenting on the Government's refusal to hold an inquiry: ". . . perhaps the Government are determined to maintain the BBC's monopoly so that they may eventually exploit it as a means of influencing public opinion in this country." June 27, 1946.

The observable fact that the Labour Government moved quickly to restore the BBC's independence of Government and Department direction did not assuage Conservative fears and resentments.

Conservative doubts of the Labour Government's intentions were deepened by Mr. Herbert Morrison's rather inept statement on June 25, 1946, that "the Government intend to do everything they can to prevent commercial broadcasting to this country from abroad."[6] This remark was challenged on July 10th by Mr. Wilson Harris, who asked how it was proposed to effect this. The lack of clarity in Morrison's statement led Mr. Harris and others to wonder if the Government intended to censor, to decide what was desirable or undesirable for people to hear "in this free country". Dissatisfied with Mr. Morrison's evasive reply to Mr. Harris, Mr. Churchill harried the Labour Minister, implying that the Government policy meant, in effect, "peacetime jamming". Nevertheless, he was unable to elicit information on how the Government intended to prevent broadcasts to Britain.[7] Ironically, Mr. Morrison's statement of policy closely paralleled a similar answer given by Mr. Anthony Eden, as Foreign Secretary, in February, 1938, when Mr. Robert Boothby had questioned the Conservative Government's policy regarding sponsored programmes originating abroad.[8]

Increasing anxiety over the Labour Government's intention regarding the future of the BBC led to the appearance on the Order Paper, June 26, 1946, under Mr. Churchill's name, of a motion calling for the submission of the question of renewal of the BBC Charter "with or without amendment" to a Joint Select Committee of both Houses. To Mr. Churchill's surprise some 211 Members subsequently signed their names to this motion, though only one Labour M.P. actually signed it. There might well have been more Labour signatures on this motion, for at one time it was reported that at least twenty Labour Members were in revolt against the

Government's decision, and the Labour Party Public Information Committee, chaired by Mr. Patrick Gordon Walker, was said to have unanimously opposed the Government's recommendation. However, only Mr. Garry Allighan and two Independent Labour Party Members signed, presumably because at a meeting with the Public Information Committee Mr. Morrison agreed to an inquiry within two years. He also announced, on June 26th, the Government's intention to publish a White Paper on broadcasting policy in relation to the renewal of the Charter of the BBC.[9]

In the House of Lords, Lord Brabazon of Tara instituted a debate with the hope, he said, of modifying the forthcoming White Paper since he had learned that once printed "the policy therein becomes sacred and you can never change it."[10] While declaring his interest as a director of Electric and Musical Industries, Ltd., Brabazon assured his listeners that he had not been briefed to speak and, in fact, did not know that his fellow directors would approve of his comments. Professing great admiration for the BBC, despite his antipathy to "women's voices singing hotted tunes, out of tune and out of time," he argued that an inquiry was merely a matter of efficient business practice. For "any first class firm would consider itself out of date if it did not have a thorough investigation into its organization at least every five years."[11] Though he was against introducing advertising on the BBC, he was opposed to attempts of the Government to prevent British advertisers from using European stations. It was, he believed, striving to live in a fool's paradise to think it possible that "we are never going to have advertisements." Britain was "no longer an island from the point of view of broadcasting. There will be stations in Ireland, Belgium, France and Holland, pouring out advertising programmes, and how can you stop them?"[12] In addition, he advocated the introduction of the Australian system, with public and commercially sponsored programmes, but focused his remarks on the need for an inquiry.

Lord Brabazon was supported in his request for an inquiry by nine Peers, four of whom favoured the introduction of sponsored broadcasting. All but one or two of them concentrated on monopoly as the principal issue to be resolved. Lord Elton, who had been a member of the Ullswater Committee in 1935, felt that that committee had "examined almost every question except the great question, the fundamental question: Is a Government monopoly of broadcasting justified?"[13] Lord Foley, pianist and composer who had a weekly programme on Radio Luxembourg, making his first speech in the House of Lords, thought it significant that Radio Luxembourg should have gained so many listeners for "the very much despised commercial broadcasting." He and Lord Brabazon outlined many of the arguments for commercial broadcasting which they and other proponents were to use in the public campaign for television in 1953.

In summing up for the Government Lord Listowel, the Postmaster-General, did clarify the method by which the Government hoped to prevent foreign broadcasts being aimed at Britain. In answering Lord Brabazon, he told the Peers that "it is possible by agreement with other Governments, if broadcasting stations abroad are under Government control, to avoid a foreign broadcast. That is what I was suggesting."[14] He reminded the Peers that "all three of the Committees that have inquired into British broadcasting . . . turned down sponsored programmes as a general and permanent practice. . . ." Though conceding that a "strong theoretical case . . . could be made out for competitive broadcasting" he thought this ignored the technical difficulty in Britain caused by an inadequate number of wave-lengths. Furthermore, even if it became technically possible to introduce competitive broadcasting, the result, he predicted, would be "an outcry from thousands of people all over the country because the programmes to which they listen would have deteriorated to such an extent." And his prophecy was no better in concluding that "I am perfectly certain that any

B

Government of any political complexion which might be in power at the time of such a decision would have to restore the *status quo* very soon after the attempt to set up a competitive broadcasting system for this country."[15]

On July 2, 1946, the Labour Government issued its first White Paper on broadcasting policy, which asserted the Government's satisfaction that the present system of broadcasting "is the one best suited to the circumstances of the United Kingdom."[16] The Government also believed it desirable to have the problems of the BBC "fully ventilated" and therefore "they are not opposed in principle to the appointment of an independent committee of inquiry. . . ." They rejected an immediate inquiry before the renewal of the Charter because of the abnormal conditions under which the BBC had been operating since the outbreak of World War II. This had meant only two and a half years under normal conditions, an insufficient time in which to form any conclusions. Sir William Haley and other officials of the BBC were opposed to an immediate inquiry partly because of the time required in preparation for a full-scale reporting of activities, and because the two new post-war programmes instituted by Sir William Haley, the Light in July, 1945, and the Third to begin in September, 1946, had scarcely had time to be evaluated.*

Though the Government recognized that the previous ten years had seen great technical advance in electronics, they felt that the research had concentrated on military uses, so it was too early to foresee the effect of these developments on peacetime broadcasting. In regard to the problem of wavelengths to be available for broadcasting, time was necessary to obtain international agreements and revise existing agreements. Finally, there was not sufficient time to permit the

---

* At least one newspaper attacked the White Paper as BBC-inspired: "Between every line of the White Paper . . . the hand of Broadcasting House can be detected. It is more an apologia than a policy." *The Star*, London, July 3, 1946.

appointment of a committee and have its report before the
Charter expired on December 31, 1946, and to extend the
Charter and licence for one year would merely make the
BBC's planning more difficult. For these reasons the Labour
Government proposed a five-year extension of the Charter and
Licence from January 1, 1947, and promised to consider well
in advance the desirability of appointing a committee of
inquiry. The White Paper as originally drafted had proposed
a ten-year Charter for the BBC. The final proposal for a five-
year extension was the Cabinet's concession to those who
wanted an immediate inquiry.

Convinced of the desirability of a single public service
corporation to direct both radio and television broadcasting,
any consideration of advantages to be gained from competition
had to be formulated within this framework. Since both the
Government and the BBC professed to be aware of the
"advantages to be derived from the spirit of competition in
broadcasting" it was stated that the BBC "is actively pursuing
a policy of enhancing the status of its individual regional
organizations." The White Paper rejected any concession to
those who advocated the use by the BBC of commercially
sponsored programmes. "The Corporation has shown no
desire to use sponsored programmes, and any attempt to do
so, they consider, would be resented by a large body of
public opinion."

In the Commons, while introducing a debate on a motion
for a grant-in-aid to the BBC, Mr. Henderson Stewart made
the key speech attacking the White Paper proposals for
continuation of the existing system.[17] He referred to Mr.
Churchill's motion calling for an independent inquiry,
pointing out that at least one-third of the Members had
indicated their support. Though the "monopoly was inevitable and right" when broadcasting started, now that it "may
become the most powerful single instrument in the formulation of public opinion" men in all countries, and "particularly
in ours" are uneasy about the future of broadcasting. Denying

that the shortage of wave-lengths any longer provided sufficient justification for continuing the monopoly, Stewart insisted that "it is into the nature of the monopoly itself, out of which all these other defects spring, that I think a penetrating inquiry is most strongly required today. . . . It is a good system for the Government! But the question we have to ask ourselves is whether it is the ideal system for the people, our people, with their highly individualist and democratic character." The very fact that controls over food, clothes, fuel and light were likely to exist for a long time made it essential "that the things of the spirit shall enjoy the fullest freedom we can give them." Stewart insisted that the establishment of separate broadcasting corporations "need not have anything whatever to do with commercial broadcasting," though he thought the latter "worthy of re-examination". Subsequently, writing in the Edinburgh *Evening News*, Mr. Stewart admitted that the Government had never, except during World War II, attempted to interfere in the day-to-day running of the BBC. Nevertheless, he urged the end of the monopoly and the creation of "one or more broadcasting systems . . . run by a commercial concern under proper safeguards."[18]

Mr. Herbert Morrison, to whom Mr. Attlee had delegated responsibility for major broadcasting policy, replied for the Government. He scored a point in noting that the Coalition Government had decided to continue the BBC unchanged and without holding a preliminary inquiry. He found Churchill's motion rather surprising because many who signed it were members of the Coalition and the "Caretaker" Governments. Had they felt an inquiry so vital they could have authorized one. Mr. Brendan Bracken, who had been Minister of Information during the Coalition Government, intervened to suggest that but for the General Election there would have been an inquiry, for it "was clearly the intention of the 'Caretaker' Government and, I think," Bracken said, "of its predecessor to grant an inquiry into the BBC." Mr.

Morrison urged caution lest they reveal Cabinet secrets and challenged Bracken's assertion.

The facts seem to be that neither Government, Coalition or Caretaker, made any recommendation for an inquiry. In May, 1943, Mr. Granville had asked Mr. Churchill if he would set up an inquiry to consider the position of the BBC, "in view of the growing tendency of the Government to utilize the services of the BBC as a Ministerial monopoly," and Mr. Churchill had replied, "No, sir."[19] The Reconstruction Committee under Lord Woolton accepted the recommendations of the Hankey Committee which had been appointed in September, 1943, to consider the future of television. The Committee had recommended, among other things, that the BBC should continue to operate both radio and television. The evidence suggests, therefore, that not until the election of the Labour Government in 1945 had the Conservative leadership any intention other than to continue the BBC Charter unchanged. This situation led the *Manchester Guardian*[20] to conclude: "It is hard not to suspect in all this the sulphurous smell of the political and commercial pit and not a disinterested attempt to secure for the country the best possible public broadcasting service."*

On the issue of monopoly Mr. Morrison denied that the BBC "is under the thumb and orders of the Government," stressed the limited number of wave-lengths as a controlling factor, and insisted that the fundamental problem is "to ensure that the microphone is controlled by some body in which the public can have confidence." He emphasized that the existing system prevented the Government from abusing their "nominal" power. "In practice, there is a clear understanding that the Government will not use their powers as long as the Corporation does not misconduct itself." He

* In the debate on July 16, 1946, Henderson Stewart noted that "it is quite true . . . that the Coalition Government . . . came to the conclusion that the Charter should be extended without inquiry." H.C. Debs. 425:1068.

assured the Commons that he would like to see an investigation before the Charter came up for renewal in 1952. An investigation "will in fact take place as soon as the international wave-length position is clearer, and we have some better idea of where the new technical developments are leading us."

Recognizing that "there are powerful and not always disinterested, voices pressing the claims of commercial broadcasting in this country today," Mr. Morrison insisted again that because of limited wave-lengths available "the number of commercial programmes which could be made available to listeners . . . would be very limited indeed, and the power of the owners of the transmitting stations correspondingly great. I have a feeling that to mix up commercial advertising with this business introduces into it an element of unhealthiness which would not be for the good understanding and good of British broadcasting, or in the end, for its quality either." He denied the need for increased revenue from advertisements either for research or for paying high fees to film stars and artistes. "The BBC has never been short of money, and is not short of money at the moment, and any Government that did not ensure that within reason it had ample funds at its disposal for research and development would be stupidly sacrificing one of our major assets." He considered present fees for artistes adequate to secure "the services of anyone who is not suffering from megalomania. We should be on our guard against interests who want to see the BBC unduly milked." The Government were satisfied that regional devolution would stimulate sufficient competition, so that apart from changes in consultation with the staff, they proposed "to keep the constitutional status of the BBC substantially as it is. We believe that the organization is still right."

Mr. Brendan Bracken also placed primary emphasis in his remarks on the monopoly issue, suggesting that the original decision had been taken before anyone anticipated the development of broadcasting. "Twenty-five years ago, few people in this country anticipated that the BBC would become a part of every home, and of almost every school, a great influence in Empire and foreign affairs and, perhaps, the most trusted newsgiver in the world." He had some generous comments to make on American radio: its entertainment is infinitely superior, many educational and other features "are truly brilliant," and it "is certainly far more courageous in dealing with controversial issues." Yet he also criticized its extreme commercialization, concluding that "we should not accept sponsored radio without a thorough inquiry into its working." The basic problem, he seemed to suggest, was that of rising costs. "I do not think that sufficient care has been taken in estimating the heavy costs of television." For this reason he rejected the proposal of *The Economist* for three competing broadcasting corporations based on licence fees and not taking advertising.[21] "The probable result . . ." Mr. Bracken thought, would be "three financially embarrassed broadcasting systems." Though many people favoured the BBC taking advertising revenue to finance television, Bracken expressed "no opinion on that subject, but it is worthy of consideration."

Mr. Patrick Gordon Walker, chairman of the Parliamentary Labour Party's Public Information Committee, expressed the views of many Members in saying, "I want to press upon the Government the need for the earliest possible inquiry that can be organized. I think there are considerable dangers in delaying the inquiry for any longer interval than is absolutely essential." Lady Megan Lloyd George agreed with this request and pointed out the concern felt by many that the wartime relationship of BBC and Government should not continue as the peacetime policy. And in reference to commercial broadcasting Lady Megan foreshadowed the position she was subsequently to take as a member of the Beveridge Committee. She commented that the Government had dismissed this possibility "almost in a sentence.

They have told us that we shall get all the variety we need, by developing regional stations. They say that in that way we shall get competition. We hope that we shall."

One of the most interesting contributions to the debate was made by a Conservative, Sir Ian Fraser, who had been a member of the BBC Board of Governors for ten years as well as serving on the Crawford Committee. Informing the House that should the Churchill motion go to a division, "I should vote against it," Sir Ian observed that he would also vote against a Royal Commission to inquire into either the BBC or the Press. He doubted the value of periodic inquiry: "It should not become a regular feature of our life to disturb a well run and deserving concern at intervals." His experience on the Board had served to convince him that the BBC Governors "have stood up against the hundred and one different kinds of pressure brought to bear on us." He did concede that in the 1930's there was too much subservience on the part of the BBC to the Whip's Office. "It was very wrong that the Governors of that time—I was one of them— should have taken that view, but things looked so different afterwards." On the question of BBC left-wing bias, a favourite point of Conservatives and one used subsequently to persuade reluctant backbenchers to support the commercial television bill, Sir Ian gave what is probably the most valid explanation of this deeply felt Conservative conviction. "For the last twenty years the Leftish view has been under-represented in our Press. Three, four or five newspapers give the other point of view to one Leftish point of view, yet the Leftish view has grown until, today, it is undoubtedly widely felt. It is a great shock to a person who has always read the *Daily Mail* suddenly to hear an organization like the BBC, something which he thinks is august, British, and much to be admired, put out a statement which he would have read in the *Daily Herald* if he knew that it existed, but did not know existed. . . . When the Press of the Left is so under-represented it comes as a great shock to this right-minded person to hear the kind of stuff that we on these benches have heard for 20 years, until we are sick and tired of it, coming out of the loudspeaker which he has paid for, and cherishes so highly. That being so, he says that the BBC must be Left. He thinks that there is a machine there, a deadly thing at work deliberately trying to propagand [sic] people in a certain direction. It is not true. What the BBC does is to represent the views of people as if you were to roll all the newspapers into one, so that you get a bit of this and that and, on the whole, a fair picture." Conceding that some United States programmes are brighter and better than some on the BBC, Sir Ian was certain that "for sustained good quality of broadcasting, there is nothing as good as our service." Further, it was not true that the BBC was established as a monopoly "almost by mistake". Three Members of Parliament, one from each Party, had served on the 1925 Crawford Committee and "that Committee deliberately chose to recommend the setting-up of this new type of public corporation."

Mr. W. J. Brown (Ind., Rugby) and Mr. Pickthorn (Cons., Cambridge Univ.) were most passionate on the subject of a broadcasting monopoly and the desirability of an inquiry. Both advocated at least the consideration of commercial broadcasting as a desirable alternative. Mr. Brown was certain that "one of the by-products of the system of commercial broadcasting is that heresy does come out over the air. . . . There is vastly more freedom," he thought, "over the American radio than there is over the British radio at the present time." Mr. Pickthorn thought there was no objection to sponsored programmes and the inquiry should at least consider this possibility.

The overwhelming sense of the debate was the demand for an inquiry before any considerable extension of the Charter and a deeply held conviction that the whole question of a broadcasting monopoly should be re-examined. Though Mr. Morrison refers to powerful pressures for commercial

B*

broadcasting, there does not appear to have been any considerable increase over that existing in the 1920's or 1930's. There had always been individuals associated with advertising agencies, or with Radio Luxembourg who urged the introduction of commercial radio in Britain. During the course of the debate, Wireless Publicity, Ltd., the London Agents for Radio Luxembourg, sent a circular to all M.P.s arguing that it was hopeless for the Government to try to prevent commercial radio. "If you closed down the sponsored broadcasts of British advertisers from Radio Luxembourg, it would merely flood this country with air propaganda on behalf of American-made goods to the exclusion of the British manufacturers."[22] And the Institute of Incorporated Practitioners in Advertising did produce in 1946 the pamphlet *Broadcasting* which made the case for a commercial system and was distributed "to all Members of Parliament, selected Members of the House of Lords, the Universities, the BBC, selected religious bodies and other educational bodies, in addition to advertising agents and advertisers."[23] However, there is no evidence either that the Labour Government felt itself under acute pressure to introduce any change in the ban on broadcast advertising, or ever gave serious consideration, despite the White Paper statement, to the use by the BBC of commercially sponsored programmes. Neither in Lords nor Commons were politically significant voices raised on behalf of commercial broadcasting. The *Manchester Guardian*, in commenting on the debate, appears fully justified in concluding "that there is no demand for commercial broadcasting in this country."[24]

Certainly at this time most of the critical opinion of the BBC seemed to centre in the ranks of the Labour Party, though the Party Leaders were then, as later, its staunch, unquestioning defenders. Labour Members had always considered the BBC to be oriented to Conservative doctrine and were now concerned lest the BBC be too closely tied to an official line. On the issue of an inquiry it is clear that support for it came from all sections without regard for political affiliation. This is not to deny that the Conservatives sought to make political capital of the issue, despite their previous stand in the Coalition Government. Even *The Times*, always a devout defender of the BBC, observed that "it is impossible to understand why the demand for an inquiry should be regarded with such suspicion and reluctance."* And Professor Harold Laski, writing in *Reynolds News*, regretted the Prime Minister's decision on the grounds that it would have been invaluable "to have allowed the available witnesses to tell the full story of the way in which the BBC's principle of maximum inoffensiveness has thwarted so much of what it could do in the field of publicity and education."[25] Publication of the White Paper did nothing to assuage criticism of the Government's decision since many shared the view that the reasons given against holding an inquiry were "logical, succinct, well-chosen—and unconvincing."[26]

With the wisdom of hindsight this whole discussion acquires importance chiefly because refusing an immediate inquiry led to further delay in extending the BBC's Charter. Had the inquiry been held when first requested by the Labour Party's Public Information Committee, the Government could have had the report, renewed the charter by 1948 while still in possession of a more than adequate majority, and the BBC would probably have remained in control of British broadcasting.

* June 27, 1946. In this connection the *New Statesman & Nation*, which favoured an inquiry, offered the explanation that "Mr. Attlee has been constantly afraid that the Labour Government would be accused of introducing Left-wing propaganda on the air. He has therefore been most careful to permit the BBC to regain all its peacetime liberty from Cabinet interference. . . . Now he feels that if the Government institute an investigation and propose any drastic change . . . it will be accused of seeking to capture broadcasting for party propaganda." June 29, 1946.

CHAPTER III

THE BEVERIDGE REPORT
AND THE LABOUR GOVERNMENT

IN ACCORDANCE WITH the commitment contained in the White Paper of July, 1946, the Labour Government announced in January, 1949, that a Committee of Inquiry under Sir Cyril Radcliffe's chairmanship would be appointed to advise on future broadcasting policy. However, Lord Radcliffe was unable to undertake this assignment because of his appointment as a Lord of Appeal in Ordinary. A delay of several months occurred before Mr. Herbert Morrison, Lord President of the Council, announced the appointment of other members of the Committee. According to *The Economist*, "this presumably was the result of an effort to secure the strongest possible committee for one of the most important administrative tasks."[1] One may also wonder if this additional delay did not reflect again the Government's feeling that there was no urgency, its unawareness that powerful opposition was already at work within the Conservative Party to prevent the continuation of the BBC as established. Finally, Mr. Morrison announced in the Commons on June 21st that Lord Beveridge had agreed to serve as the new chairman and the rest of the Committee was named. *

* The Beveridge Committee included: Mr. A. L. Binns, Mr. J. Crawford, The Earl of Elgin and Kincardine, The Lady Megan Lloyd George, M.P., Mr. J. Selwyn B. Lloyd, M.P., Mr. W. F.

Editorial reaction to the composition of the Committee was generally favourable, though one paper suggested that there might have been included a representative of the entertainment world as "some counterweight" to the educational representatives. And Mr. I. J. Pitman, Conservative M.P., wrote to *The Times* to suggest that there should be included "persons whose experience has specially qualified them in respect of selling and in particular consumer selling."[2]

Lord Beveridge lost no time in getting under way the most thorough investigation of British broadcasting ever made. The first meeting of the Committee was held on June 24, 1949, when a press release was issued inviting all interested persons and organizations to submit evidence. The inquiry lasted for eighteen months, there were sixty-two meetings of the full Committee, sub-committees visited the United States and Canada, as well as BBC installations throughout the British Isles, and some two hundred and twenty-three memoranda of evidence were submitted to the Committee. The result was that two sizeable volumes were compiled of the Committee's report and findings, and memoranda submitted by the BBC, Government departments and spokesmen for a wide variety of groups and individuals.[3] Following the practice of three previous Committees (the Sykes Committee of 1923; the Crawford Committee of 1925; the Ullswater Committee of 1935) meetings were held in private to obtain greater freedom of discussion, as well as to avoid distortion of testimony inevitable in brief daily press reports.

With the thoroughness characteristic of Beveridge enter-

Oakeshott, Mr. J. Reeves, M.P., Mr. I. A. R. Stedeford, Mrs. Mary D. Stocks, and Dr. Stephen J. L. Taylor. Mr. Stedeford was appointed on September 27, 1949, in place of Sir William Coates who resigned. Mr. Crawford was appointed on February 23, 1950, in place of Mr. James Bowman, who resigned. Dr. Stephen Taylor was appointed on March 20, 1950, in place of Mr. E. A. J. Davies, M.P., who also resigned.

prises, the Report included the broadest examination of the historical development of British broadcasting, the current situation, and analysis of the evidence submitted and, of particular interest for this study, a searching critical analysis of the monopoly issue and the question of introducing commercial broadcasting. There is ample evidence that several of the Committee members, in particular the Chairman, and many witnesses were deeply disturbed at the prospect of a continuing broadcasting monopoly. Certainly, if other inquiries had taken the monopoly issue as permanently settled, this charge could not be brought against the Beveridge Committee. "In the early days of the inquiry," reports Lord Simon, "the Chairman made no attempt to hide from us when we gave evidence his dislike and suspicion of monopoly." He continually searched for what he called the "four scandals" of monopoly: bureaucracy, complacency, favouritism, inefficiency.[4] And witnesses, whatever their proposed solutions, agreed on the potential hazards involved. Therefore, the Committee reported, "we have felt it incumbent upon us to probe more deeply than our predecessors into this main issue, not only because of its importance but because, in contrast to the evidence given to our predecessors, we found a substantial body of serious opinion challenging monopoly itself."[5]

The Committee divided those favouring the break-up of monopoly into interested groups and "Disinterested Outsiders". Those with a direct interest included: Radiowriters Association, British Actors' Equity Association, Music Directors' Association, the Radio Industry Council, the Radio and Television Retailers' Association, and the Scottish Radio Retailers. The most significant "Disinterested Outsider" proposals for ending the monopoly of the BBC came from a Fabian Research Group, a Liberal Research Group, and a joint statement from Mr. Geoffrey Crowther, Editor of *The Economist*, and Sir Robert Watson-Watt, Deputy Chairman, Radio Board of the War Cabinet, 1943-45. The two research groups wanted to continue broadcasting as a public service but emphasized the cumbersome size of the BBC. To meet this the Fabians advocated four independent corporations, the Liberals three; and while both rejected American-style commercial broadcasting the Liberals were prepared partially to finance television by permitting controlled sponsoring. The Crowther-Watson-Watt proposals centred on the evils of monopoly itself rather than size, arguing that it is "dangerous to the public interest" because of "the steady influencing of the public mind in what must be, in greater or less degree, more or less consciously, an arbitrary way," and because it "impairs the quality of the programmes."[6] Through the use of very high frequency broadcasting they thought it would be feasible to have three competing corporations covering the whole range of broadcasting in Britain.

After considering these alternatives the Committee rejected them not "because we reject the aims of these critics; very largely we agree with all these aims." The difference was one of means rather than ends. "The practical issue reduces itself to the choice between chartering three or four Broadcasting Corporations on terms requiring them to co-operate and accept Government vetoes and directions on certain points, and chartering a single Broadcasting Corporation subject to the same vetoes and requiring it to make steady progress towards great decentralization, devolution, and diversity. We have no hesitation in choosing the second of these alternatives."[7] Both critics and Committee were agreed that broadcasting should remain a public service. "The problem . . . is that of devising internal as well as public and external safeguards against misuse of broadcasting power."[8] Emphasizing that "continuance of a monopoly of broadcasting exactly on the present lines has dangers which call for safeguards," the Committee cited the mere size of the BBC; Londonization; remoteness, self-satisfaction, secretiveness, favouritism and injustice in the treatment of personnel as possible results. More urgently, they suggested that "when a sense of mission such as animates the BBC is combined with security of office it may grow into a sense of Divine Right, as it did in the case of Charles I. The dangers of monopoly are not imaginary."[9] Yet after raising most of the basic issues the final recommendation, that "the Postmaster-General should licence one British Broadcasting Corporation only to cover the whole of the ground now covered by the BBC", seemed to many to justify the conclusion that this was a very conservative document.

In all fairness to the Committee it should be emphasized that they gave the most serious consideration to the various proposals limited, perhaps, only by their conviction that broadcasting should remain primarily a public service. They examined the case for control through competing organizations and control by Parliament, which in other fields may prevent the abuse of power. It was apparent that physical limitations on broadcasting in Britain made more than the most limited competition impossible and, in any event, "if broadcasting is to have a social purpose, competition should not be allowed to become competition for numbers of listeners."[10] Similarly, it was concluded that "broadcasting should have an independence of criticism in Parliament greater than that possessed by the authorities concerned with nationalized industries such as coal, electricity, or transport, that is to say, without any Minister able to give direction in normal times as to the conduct of the broadcasting authority."[11]

Within this framework the Committee sought to meet the legitimate concern of those who feared monopoly and, above all, monopoly in any form of communication. They sought to answer the basic question: "How can a body with a monopoly of broadcasting be prevented from developing the faults of complacency, injustice, favouritism? How can it have the springs of diversity, continuing initiative, and experiment ineradicably implanted in it? . . . Can we without direct Parliamentary control prevent a chartered monopoly for broadcasting from becoming an uncontrolled bureaucracy, and, if so, by what means?"[12] In raising this fundamental issue the Committee recognized "that the achievement of broadcasting in Britain is something of which any country might be proud"; but "however admirable the past achievement of the BBC what we are concerned with is the future."[13]

To this end, the Beveridge Committee submitted one hundred recommendations to the Government and the Corporation, most of which were ignored in the subsequent discussion of the BBC's future. Of these recommendations, several might, if implemented, have gone far to meet the criticisms of those who feared monopoly and disliked bureaucracy, although they would not have satisfied those who conceived broadcasting to be primarily a commercial instrument for the sale of commodities and services. They recommended, for example, that the BBC was to have the Charter obligation to stimulate the development of Very High Frequency broadcasting so that eventually it would be possible for the Postmaster-General to authorize stations controlled by local authorities, universities, or voluntary organizations. Though the BBC Charter was to be extended for an unlimited period, subject to revocation, there was to be a review of its activities every five years by a small independent committee appointed by the Government and reporting to Parliament. The Corporation was also to submit more adequate annual reports to Parliament, with information prescribed by the Government and including an analysis of expenditures by Regions and principal services. To enable public opinion to influence the work of the Corporation, "to provide a channel, not only for popular but also for expert criticism, from outside" it was proposed that there be a Public Representation Service established, with a head serving as a Director and member of the Board of Management of the Corporation.[14] To achieve greater regional devolution they recommended that the Government appoint Broadcasting Commissions for Scotland, Wales and Northern

Ireland with a chairman who would also be a Governor of the BBC. There was to be sufficient delegation of powers, including adequate wave-length allocation and finance, to enable each Commission to develop a regional programme. In lieu of the Parliamentary control exercised upon Ministers and, through them upon the Civil Service, the Committee urged that the Governors of the BBC act collectively as "agents of democratic control". They recommended that more Governors be appointed, that salaries be increased to compensate for increased duties, and that Governors be concerned with practice and execution, as well as policy and principle. ". . . They must have the unquestioned right to look into every detail as a Minister has and like a Minister they must be prepared to defend or correct every detail."[15] In essence they sought to safeguard against the possibility of a Director-General acquiring absolute power, revealing a conviction shared by many that during both the Reith and the Haley régimes the Director-General had been too powerful and the Board of Governors too feeble.[16]

While rejecting the argument that the issue between monopoly and competition hinged upon the availability of financial resources, the Committee explored the issue of commercial broadcasting more thoroughly than had any previous committee. Though the Committee decided that "the weight of authority" in Britain was against using broadcasting for advertising purposes they felt it essential to examine the issue. *

* Those organizations and individuals opposed to advertising or sponsoring and submitting testimony to the Beveridge Committee included: the Incorporated Association of Headmasters, the Headmasters' Conference, the Labour Party, the Trades Union Congress, the Workers' Educational Association, the Educational Institute of Scotland, the Presbyterian Church of England, the Electrical Association for Women, the British Council of Churches, the Fabian Research Group, Mr. Geoffrey Crowther and Sir Robert Watson-Watt, the BBC Staff Association, the

Although permission to broadcast advertisements had never been sought by the BBC, the Licence did not categorically exclude them; it did, however, call for the "consent in writing of the Postmaster-General."* In evaluating the testimony presented, the Committee distinguished between "sponsoring" and accepting commercial advertisements. "Sponsoring of a programme means that some outside interest pays the piper and calls the tune. But broadcasting may be used also for advertisement directly without affecting the rest of the programme: an advertiser may pay for permission to insert an announcement of his wares just before or just after or in the middle of a programme . . . without himself being concerned in any way with the contents of a programme."[17]

Quite naturally and properly the principal argument on behalf of commercial broadcasting was presented by the Institute of Incorporated Practitioners in Advertising. Though maintaining throughout the controversy that the Institute was neutral, as distinct from those members who actively worked to obtain commercial outlets, its pamphlet, which had been distributed to Members of Parliament

---

Association of Cinematograph and Allied Technicians, the Musicians Unions, the Newspaper Society, and the Newspaper Proprietors Association.

Support for commercial broadcasting came from: the Listeners' Association, the Port of Plymouth Junior Chamber of Commerce, the Liberal Research Group (for television only), the British Actors' Equity Association, the Music Directors' Association, the Radio Industry Council, the Radio and Television Retailers' Association, the Institute of Incorporated Practitioners in Advertising, Horlicks, Ltd., Lever Brothers & Unilever, Ltd., Rowntree & Co., Ltd., Reckitt & Colman, Ltd., and Thomas Hedley & Co., Ltd.

* Other Committees of Inquiry had considered radio sponsoring but none had recommended as complete a ban as had actually operated.

during the 1946 debate, and its memorandum of evidence to
the Beveridge Committee were reasoned briefs for "controlled commercial broadcasting".[18] The pamphlet had been
"adopted as an official publication of the IIPA although
the preparation of it had been largely undertaken by J.
Walter Thompson Company, Ltd."[19] It is interesting that
there was no emphasis on monopoly in the case made by the
professional advertising spokesmen at that time. The 1946
pamphlet did not propose that the BBC should cease to be
"the chosen instrument for broadcasting or that official
control should in any way be abandoned. What is suggested
is rather that the BBC should make use of those provisions
in its legal structure which would allow commercial broadcasting to be carried on under certain conditions—in other
words, not the creation of commercial competition for the
BBC but the expansion of officially controlled broadcasting
with all the advantages of internal competition. . . . Broadcasting in this country is firmly under official control, and
there is no suggestion that it should not remain so."[20] In
essence the agency case was simply that commercial broadcasting "would provide industry with a powerful weapon for
sellings its goods, and that in return industry would provide
greatly increased resources, both in money and opportunity,
by which public entertainment could be improved. Above all,
however, this increased scale of operations would enable us to
compete on reasonable terms in the vitally important entertainment industry which, through film and radio, has become
a great international force, and in which our present weakness
is a national danger."[21]

The memorandum, which was written three years later
especially for submission to the Beveridge Committee,
contained an elaboration of the argument as well as focusing
upon certain aspects which it was thought might carry
political weight. Thus the need was stated for commercial
broadcasting to enhance British exports by building up a
stable home market, "a condition precedent to the develop-

ment of markets for their goods overseas."[22] This particularly applied to the manufacturers of radio and television
sets who were, it was said, handicapped by the failure to
expand television coverage, a result of the restrictions on
BBC capital requirements. To counteract those critics of
"Americanization", a synonym for vulgarity and bad taste,
the Practitioners were certain that there was "no reason
whatever to suppose that British commercial programmes
would imitate commercial radio in America."[23]

The Incorporated Society of British Advertisers, representing some four hundred firms who regularly purchased
advertising facilities, submitted the results of an inconclusive
poll of members and non-member firms. Unfortunately for
the utility of the results, only 382 firms of the 1,330 receiving
the questionnaire replied, and of these only 291 companies
normally directed advertising to the public. A majority
(58.1 per cent) favoured the introduction of commercial
broadcasting, but a sizeable minority (41.9 per cent) was
opposed. Generally it was those firms in the medical,
cosmetic, toilet, food, drink and grocery trades and firms
with American connections that tended to favour commercial
broadcasting. Three firms—Horlicks, Ltd., Lever Brothers &
Unilever, Ltd., and Rowntrees, Ltd.—presented a joint
memorandum which favoured establishment of a dual system
of broadcasting similar to that existing in Australia and New
Zealand, in which the BBC would be supplemented by a
commercial system supported by the sale of advertising time.
Mr. Cyrus Ducker, then of the London Press Exchange,
participated in the preparation of this statement, as did J.
Walter Thompson executives. Ducker feels that the testimony "carried very great weight and influenced Selwyn
Lloyd's minority report."[24] Thomas Hedley & Co., soap and
detergent manufacturers, submitted a separate memorandum
because they were not satisfied with the representative
nature of the presentation by the Society of British Advertisers. They thought that the introduction of commercial

radio would be of benefit to advertisers, the country and the
public, but somewhat cautiously suggested the establishment
of a commercial station for an experimental three-year
period.

The Beveridge Committee found the problem of commercial broadcasting the most difficult one on which to reach
agreement. In the end, a majority were prepared to leave the
issue to be resolved by the BBC and future Governments.
All but one of the members rejected the possibility of establishing any system of broadcasting which would be dependent
"either wholly or largely" on payment by advertisers.
"Dependence upon sponsors for the means of broadcast
communication is in the last resort dictated for the wrong
aims and often takes forms which public opinion in this
country would reject." They made the obvious point, too
often overlooked by those who criticize the commercial
orientation of the mass media, that "if the people of Britain
want broadcasting essentially as a public service, they must
be prepared to pay the cost of this service directly."[25] It did
not follow from this that there would be automatic rejection
of broadcasting advertisements. In fact, of the eleven
members of the Committee, only seven rejected sponsoring
or advertising in any form; the Chairman and two other
members, while accepting the principle of a broadcasting
system which was financially independent of advertisers, saw
no reason why "a public service broadcasting agency should
not set aside named specific hours for programmes admitting
advertisement. . . ."[26] They were willing to leave it to the
Governors "to explore the practical conditions under which
the means of communication which they control should be
used for the legitimate purpose of bringing would-be sellers
and would-be buyers together. . . ."[27]

Mr. Selwyn Lloyd, later Secretary of State for Foreign
Affairs but in 1949 a relatively unknown Conservative
backbencher, wrote a minority report destined to become the
most influential part of the Beveridge Report. Lloyd called

for commercial radio and television alongside a public service BBC, because he felt that sponsoring provided a method for eliminating the potential dangers of monopoly. This was to become in 1953 the nominal platform for the dedicated minority which ultimately succeeded in converting the Conservative Parliamentary Party to commercial television. Though Mr. Lloyd subsequently supported and worked with the Conservative backbench group, he apparently arrived independently at the conclusions expressed in his minority report. He found himself unable to agree with his Beveridge Committee colleagues on "the most important matter submitted to us": the continuing monopoly of all broadcasting by the BBC.[28] With three of his colleagues he had visited the United States in August and September, 1950, to observe American broadcasting. Some of his colleagues believe this experience influenced him very greatly. Certainly his report on American broadcasting to the Committee foreshadowed his ultimate disagreement with the majority. He seems to have been most interested in the number of small private stations and the variety of programmes available to listeners, revealing some indifference to the programme content. Lloyd thought that small local stations "can be used to promote community spirit and local talent and enterprises and to perform the function of the local newspaper in Britain, but rather more attractively and effectively."[29]

Lloyd also listed some of the defects he found in the American system. He cited the absence of a public service network: "it does not seem right to leave all public service broadcasting to the chances of commercial competition or the idealism of the controller of a network at a particular time."[30] He pointed out the weakness of the Federal Communications Commission in relation to programme content; the influence of advertising agencies on programme content; and the advertisements themselves. "Much of the advertisement matter is boring, repetitive, and rather offensive to British

ears. There seems too much of it, it comes at too frequent
intervals, and it spoils enjoyment of otherwise good items.
. . . I would not willingly agree to British listeners being
subjected to the full blast of USA radio advertisement. On
the other hand, I should not think it impossible to devise
rules which would make it more tolerable. Nevertheless,
advertising matter is a price to be paid, and must be faced as
such."[31]

In rejecting monopoly control, Mr. Lloyd singled out four
evils—the unwieldy size, the hindrance to technical development, one employer and excessive power. He was particularly critical of the conception "that it is the BBC's duty
to decide what is good for people to hear or to see, and that
the BBC must elevate the public taste. . . ."[32] While accepting
many of his colleagues' recommendations for controlling
what Lord Reith had characterized as "the brute force of
monopoly," Lloyd believed that "the only effective safeguard
is competition from independent sources."[33] To this end he
advocated the establishment of a Commission for British
Broadcasting with the power to allocate frequencies, licence
broadcasting stations, regulate political controversy, religious broadcasts, protect small advertisers, regulate the
affiliation of local stations to networks, and the enforcement of
standards and rules for advertising. (This proposal would
have deprived the Post Office of most of its power over
radio and television development, a secondary end desired
by many of those interested in commercial radio and television.) The Commission would license the BBC to continue
its public service functions, broadcasting the Home and
Regional Services as well as having the duty to provide
News, School Broadcasting and Overseas Services. No
advertising would be permitted on the BBC, for revenue
would continue to be obtained from licence fees and the
grant-in-aid for Overseas Services. To provide competition
in sound radio, one or two commercial corporations would be
authorized to provide national programmes. Local stations

run by universities, local authorities and private companies, and financed by advertising would also be licensed by the Commission. In television, Lloyd envisaged a British Television Corporation, temporarily authorized to accept advertisements until such time as other corporations could be licensed to provide alternative programmes. There would then be the same pattern as in sound, with a public service non-commercial television system financed by a licence fee alongside one or more commercial systems.

As an alternative should his proposals not gain support, Mr. Lloyd was prepared to accept competition between public service corporations. His primary concern was to end the monopoly, for "the evil lies in the system. . . . It involves the concentration of great power in the hands of a few men and women, and the tendency to create a uniform pattern of thought and culture. At a time when every other tendency is towards the concentration of power at the centre and a uniform society, this issue in broadcasting is of outstanding importance for the country."[34]

The Beveridge Report was submitted to Parliament on January 18, 1951, though the Cabinet actually received the Report before Christmas, and the BBC on January 8th. Following several meetings of the Governors, their reactions were submitted to the Labour Cabinet sometime around the middle of February. As Lord Simon, Chairman of the BBC, commented, "naturally we in the BBC regarded the Report as a great victory and assumed that our constitution would be continued substantially unchanged."[35]

At this time the Director-General was assured that it was the intention of the Cabinet to have the whole question of the Charter and Licence renewal resolved by Easter, 1951. However, it was not until July that the White Paper incorporating the Government's proposals was submitted to Parliament. During this long delay there were repeated questions placed on the Order Paper by Members of both major parties intended to stimulate Government action. Mr.

Morrison's reply on February 22nd to one such inquiry is indicative of the Government's lack of urgency. Asked if the Beveridge Report was likely to be debated before the Easter recess of Commons, Mr. Morrison replied: "I should not think that there was a great hurry about that. The Charter runs to the end of the year. Folks outside the House will want to think and talk about it, which they are doing. The Government, naturally, want to consider it with great care. I would ask that we should not be pushed too hard about it just now, because we are not ready."

A variety of factors contributed to this delay. The Labour Government had plenty on its plate, problems which seemed far more immediate than broadcasting policy demanded action. As a result of the General Election of February 23, 1950, the Government was returned with a majority of only six over all parties in the Commons. Though they avoided any effort to introduce new controversial measures, the Government insisted on implementing the Iron and Steel Act. The result was almost continuous harassment by the Conservative Opposition, with repeated efforts to overthrow the Government, which was actually outvoted five times, though not on matters of confidence. Additional burdens for the already strained senior Party leaders resulted from the loss of Sir Stafford Cripps, who because of ill health was forced to resign as Chancellor of the Exchequer and from the Commons in October, 1950. Ill health also plagued Mr. Attlee, who was partially incapacitated for five weeks while being treated for duodenal ulcer, and was not able to resume his duties until April 30th. Directly impinging on the Government's handling of the BBC issue was the resignation from the Foreign Office of Mr. Ernest Bevin on March 9, 1951. As a result, Mr. Herbert Morrison, to whom the Prime Minister had delegated major responsibility for BBC matters, went to the Foreign Office and Mr. Bevin nominally took over his task in charge of the BBC Charter renewal. In the few weeks before his death Mr. Bevin was too ill to be effective, although on April 10th he did meet with Lord Simon and the Director-General, Sir William Haley, to discuss Government intentions. To complicate matters still further, this was a period of intensive and bitter conflict within the Labour Party, featuring the so-called "Bevanite revolt" precipitated by budgetary requirements for rearmament and culminating in the resignations of Mr. Anuerin Bevan as Minister of Labour and National Service, Mr. Harold Wilson, President of the Board of Trade, and Mr. John Freeman, Parliamentary Secretary to the Ministry of Supply. An already difficult international situation became more distracting as the Opposition became increasingly critical of Mr. Morrison's conduct as Foreign Secretary and the Government's policy in dealing with the Korean War, the dispute with Persia over the Anglo-Iranian oil installations, the withdrawal from Abadan* and the growing friction with Egypt over the Canal Zone and the Sudan.

With the death of Mr. Bevin on April 14, 1951, Mr. Patrick Gordon Walker, Secretary of State for Commonwealth Relations, assumed responsibility for piloting the Government's broadcasting policy. Though fully sympathetic to the continuation of the BBC as the sole broadcasting authority, Mr. Gordon Walker, as a relatively junior Minister, did not have as much influence in the Cabinet as Morrison or Bevin and was hardly in a position to demand action. He was also in some difficulty with his colleagues over the Seretse Khama affair.† All these factors contributed to delay consideration of the Charter issue by the Cabinet until July.

Some of the recommendations in the Beveridge Report

* It will be remembered that on April 28, 1951, Dr. Musaddiq became Prime Minister of Persia and a bill for nationalization of the oil industry became law on May 2nd.

† Chief of an African tribe, Seretse Khama had been removed from office by the British Government following his marriage to an English girl.

aroused controversy within the Labour Party. In particular, the suggestion for establishing Broadcasting Commissions for Scotland, Wales and Northern Ireland resulted in prolonged negotiations with Scottish and Welsh spokesmen. Ultimately this produced the recommendation, credited to Mr. Ness Edwards, Postmaster-General, and accepted by the Cabinet, that members of the Commissions be selected by or be representative of local authorities. In the opinion of Lord Simon the failure of the Government to act swiftly "was exclusively due to the question of the National Regions, otherwise the Labour Government would undoubtedly have granted the BBC a new Charter on the existing lines with only minor modifications. This one recommendation alone," Simon thought, "prevented the BBC having the old, admirable and outstandingly successful Charter renewed for another ten years."[36]

In July, 1951, the Government finally issued its White Paper on broadcasting policy.[37] There never had been any doubt that the Government would accept the Committee's recommendation that the Corporation retain its monopoly position, or that the clause prohibiting advertising without the written consent of the Postmaster-General would be retained. The recommendation for a Charter with no fixed time limit was rejected and a 15-year term proposed, leaving the question of five-year reviews up to future Governments. Though the Beveridge Committee had recommended that the Government reserve power to license other authorities to conduct local broadcasting stations after consultation with the BBC, the Government pointed out that the Postmaster-General already had this power and implied that its use would depend on the success of Very High Frequency broadcasting.

The two Government proposals which were to evoke the most bitter controversy were those for establishing "national" Broadcasting Commissions, "the majority of whose members would be drawn from the county councils and the major urban local authorities," and the Treasury proposal to withhold for three years 15 per cent of the net licence revenue for general purposes. The proposal that control of regional broadcasting should be placed in the hands of councillors drawn from local authorities developed because the Government feared that the Beveridge scheme for some regional devolution would play into the hands of Welsh Nationalists. The Cabinet therefore suggested that members of the Commissions be drawn from local authorities, so that English-speaking Wales would get fair representation. These recommendations were severely criticized from almost all quarters. The Parliamentary Labour Party, in a three-hour meeting on July 16th, vehemently condemned these proposals, and the BBC Governors took the unprecedented step of presenting a formal protest before the debate in Parliament. They argued that the projected Broadcasting Councils "will introduce for the first time into the constitution of British broadcasting a system of control based upon a membership qualified by political election in the first instance." Further, their control over policy and the content of home programmes would subject their staffs to a dual allegiance. The financial restriction withholding 15 per cent of the net licence revenue would necessitate borrowing by the BBC to carry forward its programme for full national television coverage.

On Thursday, July 19th, Mr. Patrick Gordon Walker had the somewhat unenviable task of defending the Government's scheme.[38] Before a half-full house he stressed that the recommendations were not final recommendations but were designed to facilitate Parliamentary and public discussion. "We are eager and ready to listen to all views put forward during the debate and in the light of these views, to proceed with the drafting of the draft Charter and the Licence." Actually it is most unlikely that the Government were prepared at any time to accept any alternative to the BBC monopoly, whether proposed by the Opposition or by Labour backbenchers. The Government had accepted, "speaking broadly", the conclusions and recommendations of the Beveridge Committee, though Lord Beveridge was to dispute this in the House of Lords debate on July 25th. Certainly on the two major issues, the continuation of a broadcasting monopoly under public control and no commercial broadcasts, the Government took a firm position, though not exactly as formulated by the Beveridge Committee. Mr. Gordon Walker drew the inference that Selwyn Lloyd's views in the minority report "spring rather from an objection to monopoly than from a positive desire for commercial or sponsored programmes," and pointed out that even British advertisers were not unanimous supporters of commercial broadcasting. "Fundamentally," therefore, "one has to settle this matter on principle. One has to decide whether broadcasting should be controlled by those who have broadcasting interests and broadcasting interests only at heart; or whether broadcasting should be controlled as a sort of by-product by those who have other interests at heart."

In the course of his presentation of the Government's intentions, Gordon Walker was challenged by four back-bench Conservative Members. Mr. Kenneth Pickthorn wanted to know why he assumed that those "likely to make money out of the cessation of monopoly should be those who are most interested in the matter." Mr. John Rodgers questioned whether the Incorporated Society of British Advertisers were fully representative of industry or advertisers; Charles Orr-Ewing referred to the dual system in Australia where advertisements are controlled. And Mr. John Profumo challenged the assertion that the Beveridge Report had found the overwhelming weight of public opinion against commercial broadcasting.

These four men were active members of the Conservative Broadcasting Policy Committee, which had been formed on February 26, 1951, when Mr. Patrick Buchan-Hepburn, Opposition Chief Whip, sent invitations to ten Conservative Members to serve on a committee to consider and make recommendations regarding the Party's broadcasting policy. To a considerable extent this was merely the formalization of a group that had been meeting since the General Election of February, 1950, before the Beveridge Committee had even reported. According to the recollection of two of the Members, several of the most enthusiastic proponents of commercial television had been working independently and unofficially without the sanction of the Whips' Office before they finally persuaded Mr. Ralph Assheton (later Lord Clitheroe) to use his influence to get the group made "official" with the right as a committee to report to the 1922 Committee. Mr. John Rodgers, a director of J. Walter Thompson, Ltd., and Mr. Charles Orr-Ewing, of A. C. Cossor, Ltd., a radio and electronics firm, had started an informal group "to study broadcasting policy" as soon as they entered Parliament in 1950. They early persuaded Mr. Brendan Bracken to serve as chairman, but he ultimately resigned when he saw that the group overwhelmingly favoured commercial broadcasting. Apart from having some reservations about the desirability of commercial television, it was thought that Bracken's decision may have been influenced by his former association with the BBC when as Minister of Information he had supervised its operations during the war, and by his friendship with Mr. Churchill who was, at this time, opposed to commercial television.

The Broadcasting Policy Committee, as set up by invitation of the Whips' Office, included as members Lord Dunglass, Messrs. Brendan Bracken, Geoffrey Lloyd, Selwyn Lloyd, Charles Orr-Ewing, Kenneth Pickthorn, John D. Profumo, John Rodgers and Duncan Sandys, with Mr. Peter Goldman from the Conservative Central Office as permanent secretary. Bi-monthly meetings were held during the spring in which Members sought to reach agreement on a report to be submitted to the Shadow Cabinet and the 1922 Committee by May. The Committee also invited spokesmen for interested organizations to appear, including the Director-General of the BBC, Mr. Norman Collins (who had left the BBC in October, 1950, when Mr. George Barnes was placed in charge of television*), representatives from advertising agencies and the radio industry, and enthusiasts from the Conservative Central Office.

Originally there was some difference of opinion within the Committee, with Pickthorn, Profumo, Orr-Ewing, Rodgers and Assheton most enthusiastic for ending the BBC's monopoly. (Mr. Duncan Sandys and Mr. John Rodgers had served on the General Advisory Council of the BBC, where Rodgers had in June, 1949, advocated, with Sandys' support, that another government controlled corporation authorized to accept commercial programmes be established to provide competition with the BBC.) Brendan Bracken was generally inclined to retain the BBC unchanged, though he thought it possible to overcome the shortage of wave-lengths which had originally made the monopoly necessary. Mr. Geoffrey Lloyd, who had been Minister of Information in the "Caretaker" Government and a governor of the BBC from 1946 to 1949, was opposed to breaking up the BBC and was convinced that commercial broadcasting would lower standards. Ultimately the Committee members managed to agree that the BBC would be retained as a public service institution but that some competition was desirable.

By June, the Committee was able to agree on a chairman's report to be submitted to Mr. Churchill and the 1922 Committee. A majority of the committee agreed that at least for a trial period some form of competition should be introduced into the broadcasting system, both sound and television. This they considered their most important contribution. They felt that unless an alternative were introduced before the BBC had developed new wave-lengths and completed its television coverage, the monopoly might become

* See Chap. VI pp. 143-150 for a discussion of Mr. Collins' resignation from the BBC and his subsequent role in advocating commercial television.

permanent. They favoured the licensing of independent stations to develop Very High Frequency broadcasting, but if this were not possible within two or three years, the BBC should make available one of its three sound services for competitive broadcasting. The same recommendations and procedures were applied to television developments: local and regional stations were to be established, but until this was accomplished the BBC should share its broadcasting time with competitors. They also recommended the establishment of a Commission to take over from the Post Office civil servants the allotment of frequencies, as well as to exercise general supervision over programmes and advertising, a point subsequently made by Orr-Ewing in the Commons debate of July 19th. The BBC Charter should be granted for a period limited to ten years. Financing the development of the competing stations would be accomplished by accepting commercial advertising.

On the eve of the Labour White Paper debate the Conservative 1922 Committee held a meeting to thrash out the Party's policy in regard to the Government's proposals. There were about fifty Conservative Members present and of some twelve speakers all were reported as being against the continuation of the BBC monopoly except Mr. Brendan Bracken. The meeting discussed the retention of the BBC but with competing systems permitted. Consideration was given to a suggestion that the BBC be split into three separate corporations, one to develop and produce television programmes, a second to utilize medium and long-wave, and a third to develop Very High Frequency broadcasting. There was also considerable discussion of the desirability of permitting sponsoring, the particular interest of Mr. John Rodgers and Mr. Charles Orr-Ewing. However, the selection by the Conservative Party leadership of Mr. W. S. Morrison, later Speaker of the House (elected October 31, 1951) and not a rabid political partisan, to reply for the Opposition perhaps reflected the reluctance of the Party

c

leaders to concede to backbench pressure.* Although it was said that the demands expressed in the 1922 Committee by a very small group of backbenchers and the report of the Broadcasting Policy Committee did result in some modification of Mr. Morrison's speech, the result was somewhat ambiguous and, on balance, favourable to the BBC. In the first section of his speech Morrison appeared to be making concessions to the Tory backbenchers, arguing that the main issue was one of monopoly, "of which the public are daily becoming a little more irritable and suspicious" because of their experience with nationalized coal, transport and electricity. He suggested that "the climate for considering all monopolies is less favourable today towards the prolongation of a monopoly than it was before." However, he did not think "that this was in any way the fault of the BBC", and he specifically praised the BBC for its handling of political news, a sore subject with many of the backbenchers, saying, "I do not think either party has much to complain about in the presentation of political matter."

Following a lead from the report of the Conservative Broadcasting Policy Committee, Mr. Morrison warned the Government that "many of my hon. friends cannot regard the issue of monopoly as finally closed one way or another." He rejected the suggested regional commissions staffed by local authorities for the very reason that they would tend to detract from the BBC's complete impartiality. He thought that if the regional commissions were the best the Government could do to implement the Beveridge Report they should leave the BBC as it is. "They are not working too badly, and it would be far better to leave them alone." It was possible, he thought, that Very High Frequency broadcasting might open a new field, making possible both

* Woolton, *Memoirs*: "The Conservative shadow cabinet had been divided on the issue and Mr. W. S. Morrison had replied in the Commons giving general support to the continuance of the BBC monopoly." p. 387.

radio and television broadcasts by sources other than the BBC, thus a 15-year Charter extension was too long. Finally, in dealing with the financial recommendations of the White Paper, Mr. Morrison thought that the BBC should receive the whole of the net licence revenue because they needed it to catch up on developments in television, and he was satisfied "that the finances of the BBC are prudently and expertly managed." Revealing what must have been the position of the Opposition leaders at this time, he warned that if the BBC were denied sufficient revenue "either the quality of the service must seriously decline or money must be found from some other source, and this involves the disliked sponsored programme of advertising, either on sound or television, or both."[39]

Five other Conservative backbenchers, seven Labour Members and one Liberal participated in the debate and, apart from the speeches of Selwyn Lloyd, Charles Orr-Ewing, Captain Charles Waterhouse and Anthony Wedgwood Benn there was little indication in the Commons that any fundamental change was desired in the pattern of British broadcasting.[40] And only Orr-Ewing and John Rodgers were unalterably dedicated to instituting a commercial broadcasting system.

In essence Mr. Lloyd summarized his minority report, arguing that the main issue was one of monopoly. His criticisms of the BBC were quite mild as he singled out for comment that "in the higher quarters the tendency is slightly one of self-righteousness, because there is still a tendency to regard any criticism as being a sort of sin against the Ark of the Covenant." He also criticized them for what he characterized as deliberate action to discourage the growth of local broadcasting, for he was convinced that the original technical basis for monopoly no longer existed. Yet "it certainly has been the deliberate policy of those in charge of the BBC to see that only the monopoly is technically possible." On the question of sponsoring he was less than vehement and justified the conclusion of Mr. Gordon Walker that his motivating concern was to end the monopoly. He also evidenced in the debate a willingness to consider a compromise. Referring to the various suggestions in the Beveridge Report for ending the monopoly, he said, "I agree that on this matter there is room for considerable difference of opinion, because I think one can draw a line between a set of alternatives which admit of sponsorship and commercial broadcasting and a set of alternatives that do not admit of that. In my Report . . . I come down in favour . . . of sponsorship; but if these are not acceptable to the majority of the House, I willingly accept the second set of alternatives in preference to the continuation of the existing set-up." Though he saw no reason for not accepting advertising money and thought that the leaders of commercial broadcasting in America and Canada "are animated just as much by the idea of good broadcasting and public service as the people concerned with broadcasting in this country," nevertheless he favoured strict positive controls. Should competing broadcasting be introduced, he advocated a national regulatory body "with considerably more powers than has the FCC in the USA. This body would have the duty of seeing that the taste of the public is preserved and of dealing with matters like the prevention of one interest obtaining more than one private station and the laying down of policy for religious broadcasts and for political broadcasts." To suggest that a regulatory body be responsible for seeing that "the taste of the public is preserved" might seem to contradict his assertion, in criticizing the BBC, that "in a free society moral uplift should not be a matter of compulsion."

Captain Charles Waterhouse, who had been Assistant Postmaster-General from 1939 to 1941, supported Mr. Lloyd on the monopoly issue and criticized the Government and some of his Conservative colleagues for sliding over this question. "Some of us on this side of the House are not as easy about the attitude which has been adopted so far by the

Government, and by some hon. Members on this side of the House too, on the question of monopoly." He was certain that everybody distrusts monopoly. "That is true of hon. Members on both sides of the House." He also thought that the 15-year Charter proposal was an absurd policy for a Government with "a ridiculous majority of six."

Captain L. P. S. Orr centred his attention on devolution, speaking as a representative of Northern Ireland. While he favoured the appointment of national governors on the BBC Board, he assured the Commons that Northern Ireland "is against the proposals for devolution in any shape or form," fearing that the Government proposals would merely serve to bring the BBC into politics. Although later to become one of the most active participants in the drive for commercial broadcasting, Captain Orr not only made no reference to it or to the monopoly issue in this debate, but was highly laudatory in commending the BBC. "We have had very few complaints about anything, even the question of the impartiality of the BBC—and the impartiality of anything is liable to question in Northern Ireland. . . . People have begun to regard the BBC Home Service as something almost in the position of the King, above politics."

The two final Conservative speeches in this six-hour debate were made by Mr. John Rodgers and Mr. Charles Orr-Ewing, who were the initiators and the most active participants in the backbench group which had begun working for commercial broadcasting immediately following the General Election of February, 1950. Mr. Orr-Ewing attacked the notion that there was "overwhelming suppport" for the BBC monopoly, citing in evidence a *News Chronicle* poll which showed 52 per cent of the public favouring some sort of competition, and the testimony presented to the Beveridge Committee, as well as the Report itself. He reiterated the point that Very High Frequency broadcasting had rendered obsolete the technical need for monopoly and urged the creation of local radio and television stations. He believed the country would accept "some form of sponsorship in order to get alternative programmes." Therefore, he said, "the point I am trying to make is that we desire to seek a compromise between the public service monopoly at the one extreme and the free competitive system of the USA at the other extreme." He felt that "if we instituted a Commission of British Broadcasting they could, with the advertising associations, work out a code which would be perfectly acceptable to the people of this country."

Mr. Rodgers limited his remarks to the monopoly issue and merely urged that the Government look again at this question. On the basis of a public opinion poll Mr. Rodgers was certain that "there is a real difference of opinion here between—if I might use the phrase—what the best people think and what the people think."

Though he had not been successful in gaining the support of the Public Information Committee or Labour Party leadership for the scheme, Mr. Anthony Wedgwood Benn devoted his speech to a consideration of an alternative organization of the BBC. In effect he was seeking a compromise that would win the support of those in all parties who were genuinely concerned with monopoly and disliked the commercial alternative. Mr. Benn proposed "the reorganization of the BBC in such a way as to avoid many of the monopoly dangers" which had been pointed out. Convinced from his experience in the BBC North American Service that centralization was the main problem, he suggested that there be established four boards of management responsible for the Overseas Service, television, the Home Service, and Regional. The effect of this reorganization, as he envisaged it, would be to bring the individual programme planners into direct contact and responsibility with the Board of Governors. Though rejecting advertising as a source of income for the whole service, Benn was prepared to have the Overseas Service make use of advertising when they were dealing with the United States and other commercial systems. At this stage in the controversy, before sentiment in the Conservative Party had been crystallized, Benn felt that his plan of decentralization would "meet the legitimate objections of hon. Members opposite to monopoly," while maintaining intact the BBC's public service tradition.

The Postmaster-General, Mr. Ness Edwards, in summing up for the Government, contributed nothing more than a restatement of the case for monopoly. He justified it on two grounds: first, because "a monopoly which renders a social service ought to be under public control"; and second, because the proposed regional commissions would make the monopoly more responsive.

On Wednesday, July 25, 1951, there was a five-hour debate in the House of Lords with ten peers participating before Viscount Jowitt, the Lord Chancellor, concluded for the Government.[41] Of those who spoke, four peers had served on the BBC Advisory Council; one, Lord Kenswood, had been a BBC Governor; and two, Lord Beveridge and the Earl of Elgin and Kincardine, had served on the Broadcasting Committee. Though its significance was not understood at the time, the most important aspect of the debate was Lord Woolton's public and personal commitment to the introduction of commercial broadcasting, and his emphasis that this was not—at the time—Conservative Party Policy. He stressed that he had "taken the opportunity of not consulting my Leader in this House [Lord Salisbury] about what I am going to say. He told me I could say what I liked." In opening the debate Woolton devoted his speech to an extreme expression of Conservative concern lest the BBC should be used to serve Labour Party ends. It might have been thought that the General Election of February 23, 1950, which returned Labour with a majority of six, would have destroyed the utility of this bogey even among the most nervous Conservatives. But with apparent seriousness Woolton compared the role of the BBC with the Nazi broadcasting system. Just as during the war the BBC spoke for Britain, so "I am inclined to think that the German Broadcasting System spoke for Germany. I wonder whether, if Hitler had not had the broadcasting system at his command, he would have been able to capture so completely as he did the soul of Germany." He suggested that in the future, "if we had an unwise Government able to capture the BBC," this would be an obvious danger to Britain. He did not explain what would prevent a totalitarian government from taking over all mass communications whatever their structure. But he thought that "infinitely more dangerous" than outright seizure was the possibility that the "Government might use their influence through the Chairman of the Governors to secure appointment to key positions on the staff of people who would give a Party slant to the general programmes of the BBC." Woolton insisted there "is real danger" that Communist influence might capture the BBC. This horrendous disaster he thought might come about through a Chairman who suffered "from an excess of political impartiality" or was personally sympathetic to Communism. To prevent this catastrophe, Woolton thought that the BBC Chairman should be chosen by a small committee comprised of the Prime Minister, the Leader of the Opposition, and the Archbishop of Canterbury. On the specific proposals of the Labour White Paper, Woolton condemned the idea of broadcasting commissions drawn from local councils; he objected to a 15-year Charter, insisting that seven years was long enough; and he opposed the Treasury taking 15 per cent of the net licence revenue. Turning to the monopoly issue, he made explicit his dislike for any sort of monopolies, Government or private, and thought the question to be "whether there is room both for the BBC . . . and for some form of free enterprise." Specifically disavowing any Party commitment—"I do not regard this as a Party matter. I do not want to involve anybody else in my opinions . . ."—Woolton went on record for ending the BBC's monopoly of broadcasting. Instead, "within a reasonable distance of time from now, some station should be either leased or created that would permit of sponsored programmes."

In following Lord Woolton, Viscount Samuel, a member of the BBC General Advisory Council, expressed his support for three overriding principles: that the BBC should be wholly independent of the Government of the day; that it should be a publicly owned monopoly; and that broadcasting should not include programmes sponsored by advertising. On the specific proposals of the White Paper, Samuel was sceptical of the administrative feasibility of a Public Representative to criticize programmes; he approved of regional representation but rejected councils selected by local government bodies; and he thought a 15-year Charter was desirable but without too frequent inquiries. Given his interest in philosophy it is not surprising that his major contribution was to present an indictment of commercial broadcasting that was the most profound and fundamental made during the life of this controversy. He professed surprise at Woolton's proposal on the grounds that "very few of the leaders in public life have asked for the mitigation of the monopoly by the inclusion of other organizations or an organization of advertisers' programmes." Believing that the causes of contemporary difficulties may be traced to the absence of generally accepted principles in philosophy, religion and in politics, Lord Samuel challenged those prepared to scrap or ignore traditional values of British society: "What kind of civilization do we wish to live in? What sort of mental atmosphere do we wish to have around us?" This was never answered publicly by the proponents of commercial broadcasting, or considered by the nominal leaders of the Conservative Party. He observed, too, that "our modern 20th-century civilization, by the common consent of intelligent people, is already far too much commercialized by the selling of things we use and consume. These are aspects of human life which receive undue prominence in the modern

C*

age." Now with radio and television this influence would enter every home and affect "the intellectual and mental environment of every family." In directly challenging Lord Woolton and the "new Conservatives" he had recruited for Party responsibilities, Samuel asked: "Why should we, for the sake of picking up a million or two here and there, degrade the standards of our broadcasting system by diluting it with a continuous stream of commercial advertising?" He correctly anticipated that "once you let in this principle, it is almost impossible to stop it because the financial advantage is so enormous; sponsored broadcasts must, sooner or later, dominate a large part of the programmes and leave the BBC the less remunerative ones."

The Earl of Halifax, Chairman of the BBC Advisory Council and Conservative elder statesman, confined his remarks to a summary of the views of the Advisory Council. This body had approved, "with substantial unanimity," three resolutions: they welcomed the recommendations of the Beveridge Committee on monopoly and BBC independence; they disapproved the Committee's proposals for the creation of broadcasting commissions on the grounds that they would lower standards; they favoured a ten-year Charter and urged the Government to reconsider their financial policy.

Lord Beveridge, making his first speech in the House of Lords, antagonized Government spokesmen and irritated others by making a scathing attack on the Government for ignoring or watering down the proposals in "my report", and provided additional ammunition for the proponents of commercial broadcasting. He restated the Committee's objections to monopoly, insisting that "we did not want the BBC in its present form but in a somewhat different form." Pointing out "what I feel is a slight misrepresentation" of the Committee's attitude towards broadcasting, he noted that only seven members were opposed to advertising in any form, one favoured sponsored programmes, and three members "thought the ether should be used just as particular columns in the newspapers are used for advertising." There were, he felt, four essential points of difference between the Government's White Paper and "my report". Thus all the measures designed to bring progress towards decentralization had been weakened or rejected by the Government, though he certainly hoped that regional councils selected by local authorities would be dropped. The Report had proposed a public representation service and increased internal criticism, but this too had been ignored or left to the BBC Governors to implement. Their proposals for strengthening the role of the Governors to make them "effective watchdogs of democracy" had not been suitably implemented. And nothing had been done with the Report's proposal that Overseas broadcasting should have a quite different function from that of home broadcasting. These things, Beveridge concluded, illustrated a "fundamental difference of outlook. My Committee were profoundly impressed by the dangers and disadvantages of monopoly in so vital a service as broadcasting. The Government, to judge by their White Paper, are not conscious of any dangers at all. There is nothing in the White Paper to show that the Government have even read those parts of the report. . . ."

Lord Radcliffe, speaking with a background of four years on the Advisory Council, devoted his first speech in the Lords to praising the Beveridge Report for its comprehensiveness and rejecting its proposals for changing the BBC. He urged the Government to reconsider its proposed national councils and especially their selection by local authorities. He felt that as outlined in the White Paper the councils would operate to weaken the advantages gained by a unified broadcasting system. Though it was desirable, he considered, that the Governors should have as much control as possible, and therefore he favoured the option of re-appointment and £1,000 salary, practically it should be recognized that the Director-General has to make the immediate decisions. He

strenuously objected to the suggested five-year reviews—
"what I would call quinquennial assassination by review"—
suggesting instead that the Charter should be extended for
15 years with a review, except in emergencies, just prior to
the Charter expiration.

Lord Brand, a prominent Conservative and member of the
BBC Advisory Council, agreed completely with Lord
Radcliffe and suggested that it would be time enough to deal
with the potential dangers of monopoly "if and when we find
that things are going wrong—as they are not doing at
present." He rebuked Beveridge for being "too suspicious of
everything connected with the BBC" and condemned commercial sponsoring in terms comparable to those used by Viscount
Samuel as "a poisonous influence on broadcasting," which
"does spread a general feeling that nearly everything is for
sale or is somehow connected with a commercial sales talk."

Lord Chorley and the Lord Chancellor, Viscount Jowitt,
criticized Beveridge for carping at the Government and for
expecting that his report would be adopted in its entirety.
Viscount Jowitt defended the Government's financial proposal
for retaining 15 per cent of the net licence revenue largely on
the basis that they had to find money where they could and,
in any case, the BBC couldn't do very much expanding any-
way owing to the demands on materials and manpower
necessitated by the rearmament programme.

Apart from Lord Woolton's personal commitment, the
most noteworthy feature of the Lords' debate was the complete absence of support from any source for ending the
BBC's control of British broadcasting, the condemnation of
commercial advertising on the air in any form, and the
unanimity of criticism of the Government's financial proposals
and the regional broadcasting councils. Given this all-party
expression of opinion, which was generally reflected and
supported throughout the Press, it is the more puzzling that
the Government took no action to renew the BBC's Charter
and Licence.

Until his statement of July 25th, the Labour leadership would have been justified in accepting Woolton's explanation that he was being pressured by a small minority of backbench supporters of the commercial cause. In a sense Woolton's speech was a trial balloon to test public, and more important, Party reaction. He had been extremely careful to assert it as his personal opinion and to deny any commitment of the Conservative Party or the leadership. But certainly after this speech the Labour Government might have suspected that the Conservative Party professionals were dedicated to the cause, and experience might have suggested the ramifications of this commitment.

Just before the Bank Holiday close-down of Parliament in August, 1951, Director-General Sir William Haley went to Mr. Patrick Gordon Walker and urged him to complete the necessary measures so that the BBC might be freed of the uncertainty. Though Mr. Gordon Walker was completely sympathetic he was unable to persuade the Cabinet to act before adjournment. On September 19, 1951, Mr. Attlee announced that a General Election would be held on October 25th. This announcement meant that after nine months of Labour inactivity following the submission of the Beveridge Report, the future of British broadcasting was to be determined by a Conservative Government.

CHAPTER IV

BACKBENCH TRIUMPH

ALTHOUGH IT WAS not recognized at the time, the General Election of October 25, 1951, marked the beginning of the end of the twenty-five year reign of the BBC. That the future of broadcasting in Great Britain should have played no part in the election campaign provides an opportunity for speculation on the role of the electorate in shaping crucial decisions. Certainly the issue of broadcasting policy was never formulated by the Conservative Party for ratification or rejection by the voters. In spite of frequent references to the weight of public opinion, the voters, whatever their preference, were simply not consulted.

As a result of the election, the Conservatives were returned to power with 321 seats, Labour 295, Liberals 6, and other parties 3. On October 27th Sir Winston began to fill the key posts in his Cabinet. For the future of British broadcasting, the most significant appointment was that of Lord Woolton as Lord President of the Council. The Prime Minister's decision to appoint "Overlords", with broad responsibility to co-ordinate departmental policies was also a factor, because it ultimately led to friction within the Party, contributing to a series of backbench revolts, during one of which commercial broadcasting was approved. *

* The "Overlords" were peers entrusted with the co-ordination of departmental policies: Lord Leathers was responsible for co-

With the BBC Charter scheduled to expire on December 31, 1951, the Churchill Government was immediately confronted with the need to determine its broadcasting policy. To this end, the Prime Minister appointed a Cabinet committee including Lord Woolton, Sir David Maxwell Fyfe, Home Secretary and Minister for Welsh Affairs, Mr. James Stuart, Secretary of State for Scotland, and the Marquess of Salisbury, Lord Privy Seal. The first action, as announced by Earl De La Warr, Postmaster-General, in the House of Lords on November 28th, was a six-month extension of the Charter to June 30, 1952. Some Conservative backbenchers believe that this Cabinet committee was about to recommend a continuation of the BBC without any significant alteration in its Charter when it was subjected to an intensive pressure campaign by dedicated proponents of commercial broadcasting. According to the information available to backbenchers, all members of the Churchill Cabinet were opposed to commercial broadcasting except Lord Woolton, Mr. James Stuart, and the Lord Chancellor, Lord Simonds. A meeting of the 1922 Committee in late November, 1951, perhaps influenced the Government to renew the Charter for only a limited period. It was reported that at this meeting, attended by fewer than one-third of the Conservative Members, the sentiment was overwhelmingly in favour of ending the BBC's dominant position, though not necessarily in favour of introducing commercial broadcasting.

The changed temper of the Parliamentary Party and, in particular, its attitude towards the BBC and commercial broadcasting which coincided with the arrival of one hundred new Conservative Members probably surprised the Churchill Government as much as it did the Labour Opposition. In the

---

ordinating Transport, Fuel and Power; Lord Cherwell, the Paymaster-General, was responsible for co-ordination of scientific research and development; Lord Woolton, as Lord President of the Council, supervised the Ministries of Food and Agriculture.

1946–47 debate and earlier, there had been critics of the BBC and its monopoly position, but in all the previous discussion there had been little expression of overt enthusiasm, and certainly no politically significant spokesmen, for commercial broadcasting as a solution to the issue.[1] For many years there had been individuals in all parties who wanted alternative programmes, who were dissatisfied with BBC "smugness", or "stuffiness", or "timidity"; but there were few at any previous time prepared to advocate reliance on advertising sponsorship to correct what they considered to be the flaws of the BBC. During the 1946–47 consideration in Parliament of the BBC's future, several local organizations of the Young Conservatives had staged debates on the question of sustaining the BBC monopoly, or introducing commercial broadcasting. A limited sampling of these meetings suggests, at least, that there was not only no strong demand for a change in British broadcasting, but the notion of introducing commercial radio was quite vehemently rejected on the grounds that it would result in lower standards, and that instead of counteracting the monopoly it would actually result in strengthening the power of large business firms who could afford the advertising expenditures.

Even in the first few weeks after the election there was no pervasive enthusiasm within the Conservative Parliamentary Party for the introduction of commercial broadcasting. One member of the Broadcasting Policy Committee estimated that the Party was divided approximately one-third in favour of commercial, one-third opposed, and one-third on the fence or indifferent to the issue. Certainly in the first few months, and even up to the summer of 1953, there were fewer than a dozen Conservative M.P.s who were vocal and diligent advocates of sponsored television. There was certainly justification for the conclusion of a writer in an advertising trade paper that "if the two great parties are agreed on one thing it is that the BBC's monopoly must be preserved."[2]

There can be no doubt that the initial impetus, as well as

the sustained effort to obtain the introduction of a commercial alternative to the BBC came from John Rodgers, Charles Orr-Ewing, and John Profumo, all of whom had been elected to Parliament in 1950. As previously noted,[3] immediately upon their election, these men, with a few colleagues, organized an informal backbench broadcasting "Group", which provided the major pressure on the Government throughout this controversy. It was this "Group" which was the hard core of each successive Conservative Broadcasting Policy Committee. And it was the activity of this "Group" that was subsequently recognized as "perhaps the most remarkable exhibition of political lobbying that this country has ever seen—for there has been no disguise of the commercial interests involved."[4] It is no reflection on the personal integrity of these individuals, and others who were to join them, and no disparagement of their devotion to antimonopoly, freedom of choice and competition, to note that the pioneers and most of their active colleagues were fortunate that their political principles coincided with their career and financial interests. As *The Economist* commented, the whole controversy became a "soufflé of high principles and politics" and, one may add, of direct economic interest.

Certainly the background and business experience of these individuals insured their sympathy for advertising and commerce, as well as providing access to Parliament for those business interests anxious that their point of view should be considered in the formulation of Conservative broadcasting policy.

Thus Mr. John Rodgers, M.P. for Sevenoaks where the Prime Minister lived, after a brief interlude as a sub-warden of the Mary Ward Settlement and as a university lecturer, had joined J. Walter Thompson, Ltd., the largest advertising agency in Great Britain. A director of this firm, Mr. Rodgers had also been responsible for establishing the British Market Research Bureau, an organization which in 1959 attracted some public attention because of its concern that people in marginal constituencies should have an opportunity to express themselves on the question of nationalization. Some advertising men were sanguine enough in 1950 to believe that Mr. Rodgers' presence in the Commons enhanced the prospects for obtaining commercial television.

Mr. Charles Orr-Ewing, M.P. for Hendon North, had worked for the BBC television division making routine arrangements for outside broadcasts; he then transferred his activity, serving as consultant or director to a number of electronics firms, including A. C. Cossor. In resigning from the BBC, Mr. Orr-Ewing had explained, "I am greatly disappointed at the slow progress of the BBC in equipping the television service with post-war apparatus."[5]

Mr. John D. Profumo, representing Stratford-on-Avon, who had first been elected to Parliament in 1940 when he was twenty-five, may have been an exception in not having direct financial interests in developing a commercial system. He may very well have been more concerned with the political possibilities of commercial development, since he had served as a broadcasting adviser in the Conservative Central Office after losing his seat in 1945. It was reported in September, 1952, that he would visit the United States to study the Eisenhower campaign techniques and that he would "also explore ways in which sponsored television might be brought to Britain. . . ."[6]

As the campaign for sponsored television gained momentum within the Conservative Parliamentary Party, the original nucleus of activists was joined by others who shared their devotion to the principles at stake. Mr. Anthony Fell, elected M.P. for Yarmouth in October, 1951, was employed by Pye Radio, Ltd., a company directly concerned in advocating commercial television and whose chairman, Mr. C. O. Stanley, had long been one of the most aggressive proponents. Fell had been active in working with the "Group" in 1950 before his election to Parliament. Captain L. P. S. Orr, representing Down, South, after 1950, was a member of the

Executive Council of the Association of British Chambers of
Commerce, and subsequently became secretary of the Conservative Party Broadcasting Committee. To judge by his
contribution to the debate on the Beveridge Report in July,
1951, Captain Orr was a late recruit to the cause of sponsored
broadcasting, though he became an eager supporter and
subsequently became chairman of the Mobile Radio Users'
Association, an organization created and sustained by Pye
Radio, Ltd. Lady Tweedsmuir, M.P. for South Aberdeen,
elected in a by-election in 1946, was a former Governor of
the British Film Institute, a professional public relations
consultant, and a director of Campbell Johnson, Ltd., an
advertising firm. The case for commercial broadcasting was
likely to get a sympathetic hearing from Mr. Ian Harvey,
who represented Harrow East from 1950 to 1958, and was a
director of W. S. Crawford Advertising Agency, and from
Mr. Frank Patrick Bishop, elected M.P. for Harrow Central
in 1950, who had long been an effective and scholarly proponent of advertising[7] as well as serving as director of
Broadcast Relay Services, Ltd., Chairman of the Executive
Committee of the Advertising Association, and Chairman of
Morphy-Richards, Ltd., electrical manufacturers. In 1947,
before the Birmingham Publicity Association, Mr. Bishop
had advocated commercial broadcasting in Britain, suggesting
the use of local stations operated by suitable commercial
groups.[8]

These newer Members gained the support of such Conservative stalwarts as Sir Robert V. Grimston, who had
been Assistant Postmaster-General during the wartime
Coalition Government, and of such men as Sir Wavell W.
Wakefield and Sir William Darling, whose interest in the
development of increased facilities for advertising made
them natural allies for the broadcasting "Group". Sir Wavell,
who had extensive business interests in the communications
industry, was also vice-president of the National Union of
Manufacturers, former president of the London branch of the

Incorporated Sales Managers' Association, and a director of Broadcast Relay Service (Overseas), Ltd., Rediffusion, Ltd., Rediffon, Ltd., manufacturers of communication equipment, and Hulton Visual Productions, Ltd. Sir William Darling had expressed enthusiasm for commercial broadcasting as early as 1946 when, as President of the Incorporated Sales Managers' Association, he had addressed the Edinburgh branch on that subject. While the country was crying out for trade, he said at that time, the great machine of radio lay idle as far as advertising was concerned. Claiming that he knew the difficulties of selling the higher arts with soap, he posed the question: "Are we entitled to throw away this great piece of educational and selling machinery in this narrow and restrictive fashion?"[9]

An indirect result of the Conservative victory in October, 1951, was the dissolution of the Broadcasting Policy Committee which had been formed in February, 1951, under the chairmanship of Mr. Ralph Assheton. This was necessitated by the promotion of four of the original members to the Government: Messrs. Duncan Sandys, Minister of Supply; Geoffrey Lloyd, Minister of Fuel and Power; Selwyn Lloyd, Minister of State; and Kenneth Pickthorn, Parliamentary Secretary, Ministry of Education. Before the Christmas Recess a notice from the Whips' Office to "interested Conservative M.P.s" called a meeting, chaired by Mr. Assheton, at which it was decided to appoint a study group to consider and formulate a broadcasting policy for the Conservative Party. This Broadcasting Study Group included three original members of the earlier Assheton Committee: Charles Orr-Ewing, John Rodgers, and John Profumo who served as chairman; they were joined by Brigadier T. H. Clarke, Nial Macpherson, Captain L. P. S. Orr, W. A. Steward, Sir Wavell Wakefield, and Anthony Fell who became the secretary for the Group. It could hardly be said that this Study Group was representative of general Conservative thinking with regard to broadcasting. Rather, as can be seen by its composition, it reflected the attitudes of those, in the vanguard, who were committed, not only to the breaking of the BBC monopoly, but to the introduction of commercial broadcasting.

Aware that Sir Winston and most of his immediate advisers were hostile to changing the BBC's Charter, the Broadcasting Study Group initially proceeded most circumspectly to avoid any appearance of headlong clash with the Government. To this end, they were careful to have the approval of the Whips' Office and to assure other Members that this was an approved committee. They agreed to work for limited objectives and to win acquiescence, if not active support, from the Parliamentary Party by personal persuasion. Although the most active members of the Group desired the introduction of commercial radio and television, they agreed for tactical reasons on a limited programme. This at first included the modest demand for an autonomous television service to be provided by sponsors and to begin immediately by using BBC facilities for an experimental period between 6 p.m. and 8 p.m. The Government was to be urged to announce its aim of permitting an alternative programme so that manufacturers after 1954 would include the necessary facilities on new sets. To offset criticism from Conservatives who were opposed to commercial broadcasting, it was proposed that there be established an equivalent of the Lord Chamberlain, or the Board of Film Censors, to check on sponsored television programmes. They also decided to emphasize their devotion to public service broadcasting and the continuation of the BBC, focusing their argument for an alternative system on the dangers of political bias under a monopoly, and stressing the right of the listener and viewer to enjoy freedom of choice.

To minimize the danger of premature exposure, with the likelihood that opposition within the Party might be organized, members of the Group agreed to avoid any discussion of broadcasting policy with the Press, and not to disclose the existence of the Group, or any contact members of the Group might have with Ministers. They were aided throughout their campaign by the fact that Conservative Members who opposed commercial broadcasting and desired the continuation of the BBC never organized, tended not to participate in Party meetings at which broadcasting policy was discussed, and were largely unaware of the extent to which the proponents of a commercial system were organized and were constantly pressing their case with key Ministers. The Group also had strategically placed allies who kept their views before the Cabinet, possibly overstating their support within the Party, advised them on tactics, and greatly assisted in persuading other backbenchers that commercial broadcasting would be popular with the electorate.

On December 20, 1951, an informal dinner was held at St. Stephen's Club. It was attended by seven members of the Broadcasting Group, Lord De La Warr, the Postmaster-General, and Captain David Gammans, the Assistant Postmaster-General. The Group unanimously urged that the Postmaster-General attempt to have the Government make a positive commitment to break the BBC monopoly, and to establish a Broadcasting Commission which would allocate frequencies and set standards. It was intended that this Commission should have control over the BBC, as well as over any additional broadcasting bodies. It was also decided at this meeting that the Group would prepare a paper setting forth their views on a policy to be adopted by the Government. The Postmaster-General appeared to be sympathetic, suggesting that they meet again in January, and requesting the Group to submit information and suggestions to him. Over the Christmas recess several members of the Group prepared a paper, "The Future of British Broadcasting," which was printed for circulation to the Cabinet and the 1922 Committee in February, 1952.

This policy statement reflected some of the Beveridge Committee's antimonopoly case and underscored for the

Government the backbenchers' determination to end the monopoly. It opened with a disarming tribute to the BBC and an assurance that its public service functions would be maintained. The Group insisted, too, that they wanted "to safeguard the BBC from political interference and its administration from the danger of party influence." They stressed the opposition of Conservatives to all monopolies and to that of broadcasting in particular. Before proceeding to list their reasons for ending the broadcasting monopoly the Group, in effect, warned the Government that "on this issue we are not prepared to compromise." They offered a six-point case against the continuation of the BBC as the sole source of broadcasting in Britain: first, that a democratic policy could not justify a single control over so powerful a potential influence. Secondly, they brought up the theoretical danger that "the Government of the day can, if it chooses, completely control the policy of the BBC." This hazard could become real they said, echoing Lord Woolton's contribution in the House of Lords on July 25, 1951, "in the eventuality of an extreme government gaining power." Thirdly, it was charged that the huge size of the BBC had resulted in overcentralization, bureaucracy, and rigidity. It followed, therefore, that competition would stimulate technical developments and thus encourage exports of valuable electronic equipment, as well as developing artistic talents and providing some choice for the public. In general, they argued, the existence of only one employer encouraged complacency and inefficiency because employees were reluctant to challenge superiors, who were themselves hesitant to dismiss inefficient individuals who would be unlikely to find another job. Finally, the Group raised another theme which had been talked about in the advertising press, as well as in Parliamentary debates: the alleged threat of broadcasts by "uncontrolled commercial" stations on the Continent and from Eire. To avoid this invasion, they counselled, "it would be wise . . . to introduce alternative

broadcasting systems here at home which can be developed
according to our traditions and approved by Parliament."

Immediate action was imperative because if the BBC alone
were allowed to develop Very High Frequency broadcasting
and complete its television coverage during the period of its
new Charter there would be no future opportunity to introduce commercial broadcasting. "The longer the BBC retains
its monopoly the more difficult it will be to break because
the sets at present made and used can only receive BBC
programmes." They foresaw the further complication that
"it is impossible to forecast what political party will be in
power when the new Charter expires." For all these reasons,
"we therefore strongly urge that, upon renewal of the
BBC's Charter, the Government shall make it clear that the
Corporation is not to retain its present monopoly." To this
end, "and to take the BBC itself out of the cockpit of party
politics" the backbenchers advocated "the immediate setting
up of a body to be known as the British Radio Communications Commission, on the lines of similar organizations well
established in other countries." (This was an interesting
proposal because, until this controversy over the introduction
of commercial broadcasting, the BBC had never been
involved in "the cockpit of party politics", and the model
for the proposed Commission, the United States Federal
Communications Commission, was both notoriously in-
effective[10] and the focal point for intensive political pressure.)
The Commission, which was to control the BBC as well as
any additional broadcasting agencies, was to "be responsible
to Parliament through a senior Minister," the very arrange-
ment rejected by the Beveridge Committee for the reason
that it would be likely to lead to direct political interference.

The pamphlet concluded by stating that the action recommended was both generally desirable and "politically
practicable", as well as being "in accordance with the principles of a Conservative Government." It was expected that
the recommendations would satisfy the peoples of Scotland,

Wales and Northern Ireland in making provision for national and local tastes to find expression and would speed the development of television.

With the assurance of Lord Woolton late in January, 1952, that it would be some time before the Cabinet committee would be prepared to make recommendations on broadcasting policy, the Broadcasting Group decided to concentrate on gaining support within the Parliamentary Party for their programme before presenting their proposals, as outlined in "The Future of British Broadcasting," to Lord Salisbury. As a result of this missionary work, by the time Lord Salisbury, speaking for the Cabinet committee, appeared before the 1922 Committee on February 28th, the Group was able to claim that some 95 per cent of the Conservative backbenchers were concerned over continuing the BBC's monopoly. It was reported that at this meeting, which was also attended by Lord Woolton, an attempt was made to persuade the Parliamentary Party to reject the recommendations of the Broadcasting Group and to support the Government's intention to renew the BBC's Charter unchanged.

According to the recollections of some of those present at this meeting, Lord Salisbury based his and, presumably, the Cabinet's case against any alteration in the position of the BBC on four points. Though he conceded that the concept of a state monopoly, particularly one operating in the field of information and opinion, was antithetical to Conservative principles, it was thought to be unwise to introduce any change. There was, in his judgment, no demand for an alteration in the status of the BBC and the absence of any expressed public desire for an alternative service suggested that those advocating commercial broadcasting were out of touch with opinion in their constituencies and in the country. It was actually believed by many people that a competitive service would cater to lower tastes and thereby result in lowering the standards of the BBC. In any case, it was obvious that the Conservative Party had no mandate to introduce any change. In addition, the rearmament programme and the needs of export industries were absorbing the steel and other materials which would be required were the Government to authorize the construction of additional broadcasting facilities. Finally, the Government felt that both the international and domestic situation demanded the maximum in national unity, and this proposal for commercial television would introduce an irreconcilable controversy. Therefore it would constitute a major political blunder that outweighed any theoretical commitment to the antimonopoly principle. Lord Salisbury seemed personally to consider the hazard to national unity in a time of crisis the most serious objection to any proposal for altering the pattern of British broadcasting.

Lord Woolton, ostensibly present to support his Cabinet colleague, contributed the suggestion of two additional dangers of change. There was, he is reported to have said, the possibility that the Communist Party would buy broadcast time and therefore gain an advantage from commercial television. And, similarly, the Co-operative movement would undoubtedly become commercial sponsors with the inevitable result of weakening and ultimately destroying the small shopkeeper. Obviously, after the Lords' debate on July 25, 1951, when he had been concerned that the continuation of the BBC as the sole broadcasting authority might mean its capture by an "unwise Government", Lord Woolton had acquired a new insight into potential dangers.

The Broadcasting Group was not persuaded by the points made by Lord Salisbury or by Lord Woolton. Instead they drew up a detailed refutation of the arguments presented, and circulated this among their colleagues. It was denied, for example, that lack of capital resources need inhibit development of a new service, or that it was an adequate explanation for the failure of the BBC to develop Very High Frequency broadcasting. They noted that the Corporation had managed to find adequate resources to develop and extend the coverage of the Third Programme, "Haley's pet project", and that the BBC overestimated the cost of competitive VHF stations and television facilities. In addition, it was claimed that the Radio industry was not fully occupied with defence work and that they had plenty of capacity for producing all the necessary components for an additional service, a factor which would also redound to the advantage of British export trade.

So far as public reaction was a factor to be considered, the Group insisted that the Press was not a reliable barometer of opinion because of its vested interest in preventing the development of a competitive advertising medium. It was claimed that public opinion poll figures suggest that in 1951, 52 per cent of the people were critical of the BBC, and some 66 per cent thought that the BBC would be improved by competition. They did not think there would be an irreconcilable controversy since they were not advocating any limitation on the BBC's present services, but merely proposing that the public be given additional service to be paid for commercially. There was no evidence to suggest that the public resented being given additional services, especially when not paid out of licence fees or direct taxes. Certainly the backbenchers felt that they were better able to judge the real views of their constituents than were either the Press or the Cabinet.

Following this meeting, the 1922 Committee appointed a small subcommittee under the chairmanship of Mr. John Profumo to negotiate with the Government. Early in March, Lord Salisbury moved to the Commonwealth Relations Office and Lord Woolton assumed responsibility for formulating the Cabinet's broadcasting policy. This step may have smoothed the way for the compromise, suggested by the subcommittee and included in the White Paper, published May 15, 1952, which confined the breaking of the BBC monopoly to television alone.

As a result of the untiring efforts, careful planning, and

successful proselytizing by the Broadcasting Group, re-
enforced by strategically placed allies, the Conservative
Government included in its White Paper on broadcasting
the mild, trial balloon promise ". . . that in the expanding
field of television provision should be made to permit some
element of competition when the calls on capital resources at
present needed for purposes of greater national importance
make this feasible."[11] Innocuous and cautious as many
interpreted this White Paper to be,* it nevertheless became
the irrevocable commitment of the Churchill Government to
commercial television. At the time, however, many believed
that this concession had been considered rather unimportant
by the Cabinet and little more than another general licence
to harry those nationalized industries which couldn't be
denationalized. Analysing developments after May 15th, one
may observe how skilfully those interested in obtaining
commercial television manipulated events and pressure to
keep the Government committed to what had at first appeared
to be no more than a feeble, half-hearted gesture to a rather
persistent Party minority. For although there had been a
steady increase in the number of Members who were
sympathetic to commercial broadcasting or were persuaded to
go along in opposition to "monopoly", they did not in 1952,
if ever, represent a majority of the Parliamentary Party.

This increased support would probably not have won over
the Cabinet had it not been for the guiding genius of Lord
Woolton, President of the Council. In effect, Lord Woolton
served as Cabinet representative and spokesman for the
Broadcasting Group, and his words were bound to carry
unusual weight with the Prime Minister because of his part
in restoring Conservative morale and re-building the Party
machine. While creating the impression of reluctant capitu-

---

* Thus, *The Annual Register*, 1952, commented: "The White
Paper amounted to a vote of confidence in the BBC, and in so far as
a 'Trojan horse' had been introduced into the citadel of Portland
Place it might be dismissed as 'a very little one'." p. 38.

lation to backbench pressure.* Woolton had in fact been opposed to the BBC even before assuming the direction of the Conservative organization. He had long determined to break its hold by introducing sponsored programmes.†

Lord Woolton had taken over the Party Chairmanship on July 1, 1946, entering party politics formally for the first time because of his determination to save the country from socialism, which he thought "was invading the strongholds of private enterprise almost without hindrance or protest. It seemed to me that the business community had fallen into a dangerous and careless state of mind. I saw the initial stages of what might become a Servile State and the public was accepting it as inevitable. I knew that something must be done by someone to rouse the country to the dangers that beset it."[12] Explaining how he happened to surrender his political independence, Woolton wrote, "I was so shocked at the prospect of the new Britain under nationalization that immediately it became clear that the Government of Mr. Churchill was defeated I wrote to him expressing my regrets and asking him if he would be good enough to honour me by allowing me to join him in the Conservative Party."[13]

In furtherance of his major aim for restoring the Conservative Party to power, Woolton completely reorganized the Central Office and the Party organization, in the process also vastly increasing the power of the Central Office. As he said,

* In an interview with the author on November 17, 1958, Lord Simon of Wythenshawe recalled Woolton's telling him: "I don't like this, but I'm afraid the pressure is too great to resist." And in his book, *The BBC from Within*, Lord Simon writes: "A member of the Cabinet said to me that the pressure was overwhelming." p. 42.

† Interview, December 4, 1958. And on July 1, 1954, in the House of Lords, Woolton said: "Before the question became a matter of Government policy, I arrived at the conclusion (it was a personal conclusion) that a monopoly of control over such a new, expanding and powerful force as television was a dangerous thing to maintain. . . ." H.L. Debs. 188:87.

this "had to be done because after 1945 there was no organization. I had to rebuild it from scratch."[14] As a result of this
rebuilding, professional advertising and public relations
men became key figures in the Central Office, rapidly improving techniques and strengthening reliance on a manipula-
tive approach to politics. Thus Mr. E. D. "Toby" O'Brien
was temporarily released from his public relations duties
for Rootes Motors by Sir William Rootes to assist the
Conservative campaign, and he was joined by Messrs. Brian
Willis, John Profumo, and Colin Mann. Miss Elizabeth
Sturges-Jones was appointed Women's Press Officer. "Public
relations officers had been allocated to every area of the
country by Lord Woolton. The publicity department provided a round-the-clock service for newspapers of all shades
of opinion. Every technique of persuasion was within
the publicists' arsenal" including touring cinema-vans, the
launching of some two hundred and forty constituency maga-
zines, some twenty-four million leaflets attacking the Labour
Party, and a national poster campaign—"the biggest organizational job in billposting ever attempted in Britain."[15]

It was Woolton's influence, too, that was behind the
considerable increase in the number of prospective candidates
drawn from advertising, public relations, and business. As
phrased by Lord Woolton, "I democratized the Party. We
had to get men with brains and not just money or position
to stand for Parliament. I eliminated entirely the need for
Members' contributions to constituency parties. We left
nothing to chance. We held schools for Parliamentary
candidates, trained them in presentation and laid down the
line."[16] This change constituted in truth what Mr. Angus
Maude, former Conservative M.P. and Central Office
official, characterized as "a silent revolution". Most of the
new M.P.s, said Maude, "came from the professions or
from business, some of them being former elementary
school boys who had built up businesses of their own. . . ."[17]
These "new Conservatives," many of them "young men on

the make," were eager to obtain financial rewards and the hallmarks of status. They were bitterly hostile to socialism, which they interpreted as limiting individual opportunities for personal advancement. Perhaps it is not surprising that they tended to be almost as contemptuous of the authority of the elder statesmen of the Conservative Party, whom they considered to be leaders of another generation, and whose policies of the 1920's and 1930's they considered, with the wisdom of 1950, to have been disastrous and, in any case, without political appeal. "Young men and women began to sense," wrote Woolton in his *Memoirs*, "that there really was a new Conservatism more practical in its outlook and therefore safer than the current Socialist practices. It began to be widely sensed that Socialism had failed and brought the country to the very verge of bankruptcy. The British people had come to realize the fact that their living was in danger."[18] This younger generation of Conservative M.P.s felt that they represented majority sentiment among the Conservative voters who wanted to end socialism and egalitarian notions, and that they reflected as well the mood of the country generally. Thus they felt, as one of them expressed it, that those Conservative spokesmen who opposed commercial television were "not the intellectual leaders of the present-day Party. They have no influence with the Members who came into Parliament after 1945."

With the Conservatives' return to power in October, 1951, the Prime Minister offered Woolton his choice of any Cabinet post. Because he was in the House of Lords he could not become Chancellor of the Exchequer, so he chose to hold again the office of Lord President of the Council. It is of interest that in his *Memoirs*, Lord Woolton comments that "the Lord President is able to greatly influence policy through the operation of Cabinet committees; such work behind the scenes was much more attractive to me than the more obvious role and the power that comes from making parliamentary speeches."[19] Woolton also retained the chairmanship of the

Conservative Party organization. To serve as his right-hand man, he hired Mr. Mark Chapman-Walker, who had advertising and public relations experience and whose enthusiasm for sponsored broadcasting had been sharpened by observation in the United States, where for a time he had served as secretary to the Combined Chiefs of Staff. In pursuit of a civilian career, Chapman-Walker first, as a Socialist, unsuccessfully sought a position with the Labour Party before applying to Lord Woolton at Abbey House.[20] Within a few months of joining the Central Office, Chapman-Walker took over from Lord Woolton the task of directing the Party's propaganda. His favourite contribution was the *Popular Pictorial*, a popular magazine which presented the Conservative political case by means of strip cartoons and "cheese cake" and featured a bathing beauty on the cover. In the judgment of his former employer, "there is no doubt he is the greatest political propagandist in the country."[21] It was Chapman-Walker who persuaded Lord Woolton of the desirability of televising the Party Conferences and subsequently arranged for the appearance of personality types appropriate to the "new image" of the Conservative Party. Perhaps this experience influenced his judgment that, by 1964, three properly staged television productions could win a General Election in Great Britain.[22]

After 1951, Chapman-Walker served as secretary to the Conservative Parliamentary Broadcasting Committee and devoted practically his full time at the Central Office to promoting sponsored television.* In his judgment the achievement of commercial television was the idea and the complete operation of the Party professional at the Central Office. "All the top leadership of the Party was opposed," he recalled, "with the exception of Lord Woolton. We couldn't have got our programme through without him."[23]

* In 1955, Mr. Chapman-Walker became Joint Managing Director of the *News of the World*; he later became a Director of Television Wales and West, one of the commercial programme companies.

Woolton's statement in the House of Lords debate of July 25, 1951, proclaiming his support for commercial broadcasting was not only a tremendous morale factor for the backbench "Group", but assured the professional staff at the Conservative Political Centre that they had his tacit approval for their work. Throughout the months they provided a steady flow of arguments and tactical suggestions designed to gain support within the Parliamentary Party and to counteract the arguments of the opposition. It is an interesting commentary on the role of a party bureaucracy that throughout the controversy over commercial television the professional staff was not only well in advance of Party rank-and-file opinion, but operated to commit the Party leadership in the Commons to more advanced positions.

Contributing to the success of the Broadcasting Group was the undeniable fact that throughout the months of controversy the Churchill Government was in serious trouble. General economic conditions did not favour the Government and they had been unable to reverse inflationary trends that were compounded by the rearmament programme. Writing in January, 1952, Mr. L. S. Amery, former Conservative Minister and close friend of Sir Winston, warned of "the imminent prospect of economic breakdown. If we fail to avert that breakdown both our rearmament programme and social welfare go by the board. . . . At home inflation is in full canter and unless sharply curbed, might at any moment break into a headlong gallop. We shall be down £400 million or more, on the last six months' balance of payments. Nothing short of the most drastic measures can avert national bankruptcy and the break-up of the sterling area before the end of 1952. . . ."* In an effort to prevent such dire conse-

* *The Times*, January 1, 1952. It was also during this period that the President of the United States Chamber of Commerce, Dechard A. Hulcy, in an address to the New York Rotary Club, urged more help for Britain and the Conservative Party. *New York Times*, December 21, 1951.

D

quences, Mr. R. A. Butler, Chancellor of the Exchequer,
announced on January 29th an extension of the austerity
programme, including further cuts in travel allowances and
imports, additional charges for the health service, and a cut-
back in the supply of cars and commercial vehicles for home
use. None of these measures were popular with middle class
Conservative voters, but their bitterness was compounded
as it became apparent that the October victory was not
producing a sweep-out of Labour legislation, and that there
was in fact no significant change and no dramatic legislation
proposed. Actually, the first session of Parliament ended with
no major legislation, apart from the Finance Act, and the
most important measure was the Defamation Bill sponsored
by a Labour M.P., Norman H. Lever. Worse than this for
those who had campaigned on "free enterprise", and a policy
of "setting the people free", eliminating controls and providing opportunity, many backbenchers believed the Government was too inclined to carry on Labour Government
policies, or alternatively, that they were too much controlled
by their civil service advisers.* It was widely believed, for
example, that the Prime Minister was opposed to denationalization of both steel and road transport.† The intensive drive

* An editorial in *U.S. News & World Report*, on December 14,
1951, stated that: "Political observers in London are asking
whether even Winston Churchill will be able to lead Great Britain
away from Socialism. *Before the election*, Churchill seemed a dyed-
in-the-wool Conservative. *Since the election*, it's almost as if
Churchill were a captive Socialist. He licked the Socialists at the
polls, but he can't shake off their policies." Citing the arms slow-
down, import cuts, food subsidies, belt tightening, and business
controls as "left-wing Socialist" ideas which had not yet been
swept out, the writer observed that the "Odds are against Churchill. . . ." on his promises to denationalize steel, lower taxes, and
give private enterprise more of a chance.

† Lord Woolton wrote in his *Memoirs*: "Repealing legislation
with a majority of sixteen is an unwelcome process, and especially
so when the ranks of labour . . . had continued to give it every

of the Conservative proponents of commercial television thus coincided with accusations by constituency associations that the Government was betraying Conservative campaign pledges and the ideals of free enterprise. There is little doubt that much of the effectiveness of the campaign against the BBC monopoly was due to the desire of Conservative backbenchers to make some positive gesture in the direction of competition and private enterprise. The BBC Charter loomed as one thing at least that could be changed.

The Prime Minister was out of touch with the rank-and-file Members who in turn thought of him as representing another generation and tradition, and who believed that he was largely indifferent to domestic issues. He had remained in public life, as he told the electorate during the campaign, because he thought he might make an important contribution to a lasting peace settlement. "I pray indeed," Sir Winston had said, "that I may have this opportunity. It is the last prize I seek to win." And it was concern with the cosmic issues of relations with the Soviet Union and the atom bomb which were his preoccupation throughout his last period in office. Sir Winston had carried into his peacetime Government his wartime practice of seeing only members of the inner Cabinet, or the "Overlords". He rarely bothered to consult or even to have general conversation about departmental matters with other Ministers. This irritated many of the backbenchers because they thought that "decisions were taken with the 'Overlords' and we didn't even consider them

---

support. . . . Mr. Churchill himself, who had been heavily committed by his own speeches in the past on the nationalization of the railways, was not primarily interested in this part of the programme of reversing previous legislation, although—fulfilling his election promises—he gave every encouragement to his colleagues to carry out those aspects in which the public interest was involved." pp. 378-379.

to be Conservatives!"* Ministers were antagonized because, in Lord Woolton's account, "in spite of all his vast experience in different offices of Government he gave very little guidance to his younger colleagues, until some issue became a matter of contention in the Press or in Parliament; many of them felt somewhat aggrieved by this."[24] They particularly resented Sir Winston's reliance on Lord Cherwell who "provided irritating facts and statistics in graph form which the Prime Minister could understand without much labour. The fact that Lord Cherwell provided the statistics about everybody else's department inevitably annoyed other Ministers, including me. . . ."[25]

On the specific question of the BBC's future Mr. Churchill tended to be indifferent. He didn't like commercial television, which he is said to have referred to as the "tu'penny Punch and Judy show," but he was also at least mildly hostile to the BBC for what he considered the Corporation's responsibility for denying him broadcasting opportunities in the 1930's. It is also likely that he, too, may have held the BBC partially responsible for the Conservative defeat in 1945, a defeat which he took as a personal rejection.† There is general agreement among all those most directly involved that had Sir Winston felt strongly and wished to do so he could have quashed the backbench movement for commercial television, just as in a meeting of the 1922 Committee he had brushed off Lord Hailsham's demand for implementation of the Tory pledge to restore the university seats. Instead he first ignored

* It is also of interest that the proportion of peers in the Churchill Cabinet was six out of sixteen, "the highest for any government in this century." Peter G. Richards, *Honourable Members*, p. 213.

† Certainly many Conservatives believed that the BBC had contributed to their defeat. It was reported, for example, that in November, 1945, Captain David Gammans "told the Central Council of the Conservative Party that the BBC was to some extent responsible for the result of the recent General Election." *The Sunday Times*, March 31, 1946; see also pp. 30-31, Chapter II.

the pressure and, according to some, refused even to read the reports submitted by the Broadcasting Committees. However, in replying to Mr. Herbert Morrison on June 19, 1952, he supported the basic concession: "the longer I have studied this matter and watched its development in the past few months the more confident I am that the present complete monopoly should not continue."

In what was primarily an internal party struggle, allies were indispensable for the backbench group, especially because the really important persuasion took place at private committee meetings, conversations at dinners, in the House of Commons' smoking rooms, and in the clubs. Lord Woolton's active support was, of course, invaluable but his tireless efforts were bolstered by others who sympathized with the commercial cause. Several of the Broadcasting Group gave high praise to the work of Mr. Ralph Assheton, who had been chairman of the Conservative Party from October, 1944, to 1946. It is possible that his interest in the broadcasting issue had been aroused by the discussions at a meeting he convened in London on October 5, 1945, of the 200 defeated Conservative candidates. In conducting a post-mortem of this disaster there were expressions of belief that the BBC's handling of political news had played a part in creating the overwhelming vote for the Labour Party. It will be remembered that Mr. Assheton had served as the first chairman of the Broadcasting Policy Committee in 1951, and had been instrumental in getting the Whips' Office to issue the initial invitations. Helpful also was Mr. James Stuart, Secretary of State for Scotland, who had been a Government Whip from 1935 to 1945, and Opposition Chief Whip from 1945 to 1948. A staunch supporter of the backbench demands in this instance, he is thought to have exerted considerable influence, in a quiet fashion, with Conservative Members. The Assistant Postmaster-General, Captain David Gammans, despite ill health, was a tireless worker for commercial broadcasting, counteracting what was considered by the Group to be the lukewarm attitude of the Postmaster-General, Lord De La Warr. Captain Gammans had declared his detestation of the BBC monopoly as early as June 29, 1944, emphasizing that although "I do not want to do away with the BBC. . . . I want to see some form of commercial broadcasting in this country as well."[26] Though he was to die before receiving adequate recompense for his devotion, it was Captain Gammans who carried the burden of defending the Government's case in the House of Commons, who spent hours consulting and advising the Broadcasting Group, addressed Chambers of Commerce and advertising associations, and spent week-ends at his country home encouraging the handful of devoted advocates.

It was this complex of forces, personalities, and interests within the Conservative Party from 1951 to 1955 which, combined with the Government's small majority over the Opposition, rendered the Government vulnerable to determined backbench revolts. There were a whole series of measures, of which commercial television was only one, which were forced upon the Government. Thus Mr. Enoch Powell, M.P. and member of the Conservative "One Nation" group, writing in *The Spectator* refers to "Members who forced reluctant governments to denationalize steel and road transport, to break the BBC monopoly and to end the Supplies and Services Acts. . . ."[27] The leaders in many of these revolts were members of the "One Nation" group which included among others Iain Macleod, Angus Maude, John Rodgers, Enoch Powell, and Edward Heath, all of whom were elected to Parliament in 1950. Initially serving as a kind of "brains trust", producing statements of the modern Tory approach, they quickly assumed important roles in the Parliamentary Party and after 1951 several became members of the Government. At one time members of this group held four Party chairmanships plus several vice-chairmanships; at least one, Iain Macleod, was a Minister (of Labour and National Service) and Edward Heath became Chief Government Whip. This obviously enhanced their influence and because they had formulated policies on many issues they could almost always take the lead in any committee. As one of them remarked, "one couldn't exaggerate the importance of a coherent group that knows what it wants, where it is going, and is determined to succeed." In addition to the denationalization of steel and road transport and John Rodgers' role in achieving commercial television, members of the "One Nation" group are credited with taking the initiative in forcing the Government to act in a number of other instances: the withdrawal of the first White Paper on Transportation in May, 1952, when the Minister, J. S. Maclay was forced to resign and a second White Paper was produced in July, 1952; the repeal, in November, 1952, of the crucial clause nationalizing development rights in the Town and Country Planning Act; and the Crichel Down Case and the resignation of Sir Thomas Dugdale as Minister of Agriculture and Fisheries. In November, 1953, twenty-five Conservative M.P.s signed a protest against talks with Egypt, and on the eve of the Lords' debate on commercial television in November, 1953, Sir Winston was bitterly attacked in the Commons for the Government's decision to refuse a pension increase to World War I officers.[28]

It is a very complicated task to attempt to explain the circumstances in which Conservative backbenchers are able to influence, or even to force the capitulation of a Government. One may doubt the thesis that "backbench pressure can be decisive only when the Government is already weak."[29] In general, however, backbench influence is likely to increase when the Government's majority is not too large, as from 1951 to 1955. The rebels' tactical position is strengthened when there is a continuing prospect of the Party's electoral success, so that the Government is reluctant to antagonize any sizeable group or to create an impression of party disunity. Obviously, too, the rebels must gain either a sizeable following among members of the 1922 Committee, or insure that they remain passive, indifferent, or disorganized. With no strong feelings aroused by a particular issue, it is likely that many Members will be sympathetic to their fellows who have the temerity to challenge the authority of the Party leaders. Such natural sympathy for revolt was probably enhanced during this period by the social, psychological and philosophical distance which was felt to exist between many Conservative Members and their leaders in the Government.

CHAPTER V

THE OPEN CONTROVERSY

PUBLICATION OF THE Government's proposals for the future of British broadcasting in May, 1952, brought into the open what had been an intraparty struggle conducted behind closed doors. The White Paper opened with a discussion of the issues of monopoly and sponsored broadcasting and, while far from being explicit, it was generally interpreted by Press and public as being a commitment to introduce commercial television some time in the future. Noting that previous Licences had not themselves established the Corporation as the sole broadcasting authority, though all previous Governments had followed this policy, the Government announced their decision "to propose alternative arrangements." They recognized "that this effective monopoly has done much to establish the excellent and reputable broadcasting service for which this country is renowned and that the BBC have become an important part of the structure of our national life." Therefore the new Charter and Licence to be issued for a ten-year period would ensure that the BBC continue on the existing basis. Since the Government would be "most unwilling" to see any change in the policy of the BBC towards sponsoring or accepting advertisements, the restriction on broadcasting commercials without the consent of the Postmaster-General was to be continued. Having decided to propose "some element of competition" in the

D*

field of television, the Government promised that the BBC "must clearly have first claim when labour and materials become available" in order to provide adequate national broadcasting services, and that Parliament should have full opportunity to consider the conditions under which the new system would operate. Anticipating the possibility of abuses, and reflecting criticisms within the Party, it was suggested that a controlling body would be required to exercise supervision over programme content "and for advising on appropriate matters." It was also made explicit that "the new stations would not be permitted to engage in political or religious broadcasting." Conceding that the BBC had been prevented from developing its television coverage and introducing Very High Frequency broadcasting by Government-imposed limitations on capital investment, the Corporation was to be authorized to borrow up to £10,000,000 for capital expenditure.

Apart from this section of the White Paper, the other recommendations were unexceptionable, although the decision to continue the Labour Government's proposal for withholding 15 per cent of the net licence revenue for another three years and the plan to have Governors selected by a committee consisting of the Speaker, the Prime Minister, and Leader of the Opposition, the Lord Chief Justice, and the Lord President of the Court of Session were subsequently attacked and the selection committee proposal was later discarded by the Prime Minister.

A two-day debate, on May 22 and 26, 1952, in which twenty-nine peers participated, was precipitated in the House of Lords by Lord Reith, who had been the chief executive of the BBC for sixteen years.[1] Though he expressed doubt that the Government would pay any attention to what was said in the debate, his conscience and his interest in the institution he had virtually created convinced him of his responsibility. Lord Reith excoriated the Government for its "clever" document—"One can imagine the stresses and strains, the pullings and pushings behind the scenes, arguments and counter-arguments, drafts and redrafts." Most of his speech was devoted to criticizing proposals for various administrative changes: the possibility of two Directors-General, the National Councils, and the intention of withholding 15 per cent of the net licence revenue. Then he turned to the crucial issue of a competitive system. Pointing out that "there is no mention of sponsoring in the whole Paper," he assumed the income guarantee to the BBC meant that any competitor would have to raise finances somehow. "Have the Government any other means in mind? If not, why is sponsoring not mentioned?" Lord Reith also asked for clarification of the timing of the new service. Did the White Paper mean that there would be "no sponsored television till the BBC has finished its television coverage and has also introduced VHF?" In his peroration Lord Reith accused the Government of seeking to scuttle and betray a broadcasting system which had won the respect and admiration of the world, and without presenting a single reason for this change. "A principle absolutely fundamental and cherished is scheduled to be scuttled. It is the principle that matters, and it is neither here nor there that the scuttling may not take place for years." Somebody, he said, introduced Christianity into England, "and somebody introduced smallpox, bubonic plague and the Black Death. Somebody is minded now to introduce sponsored broadcasting." Small wonder that the Lord De La Warr was moved to remark, "I admit that I could wish . . . that he had felt more able to give his blessing to our proposals a little more warmly than he did." In setting the tone which was to characterize all subsequent public discussion of this issue, Lord Reith urged the Government to think again: "Need we be ashamed of moral values, or of intellectual and ethical objectives? It is these that are here and now at stake."

Viscount Samuel, elder statesman of the Liberal Party, expressed general agreement with the argument of Lord

Reith and condemned the White Paper for its evasiveness in treating the issue of sponsoring. ". . . I think we are entitled to know definitely from the Government today, in short and simple terms, whether they are in favour of sponsored television or not. It is here implied. It is taken to be a fact by the Press and by public opinion. But it is not asserted. . . ." He thought the Government was probably in favour of it, but did not wish to say so, "for they feel some coyness, some diffidence, some shyness." He correctly estimated that the equivocal statement reflected the struggle within the Conservative Parliamentary Party and that the Government sought to avoid definite commitment since there were no resources available for immediate development of a competing system. Nevertheless, "the principle of sponsored broadcasting is clearly admitted in the White Paper" and must be opposed now. Though he criticized some of the administrative suggestions, Lord Samuel concentrated his attack on the central issue and urged the House to "express itself in no qualified terms and say that we are against compromise of any sort on this question of advertisers' programmes."

The Earl of Listowel, Postmaster-General in the 1945 Labour Government, found reassurance that the Government had at least intended sound broadcasting to remain uncommercialized and hopefully anticipated that lack of capital and equipment ruled out commercial television "in the near future." He found it "something of a relief to many people that the Government have listened to the wise counsel of the noble Earl, Lord Halifax, and the noble Lord, Lord Brand, and many others of their less doctrinaire supporters, who strongly urged them in past months not to introduce forthwith commercial broadcasting." He spoke for the Labour Party in opposing its introduction not because of a theoretical objection to breaking the BBC's monopoly, but from a conviction "that it would soon reduce the standards to the lowest common denominator of taste." He did not believe that any kind of supervising authority would be able "to interfere with the normal commercial practice that has debased the currency of broadcasting wherever it has been left to private enterprise." If local authorities or the universities wanted to have broadcasting stations, their requests should be considered when technical developments and resources made this feasible.

The fourth attack on the Government came from the Earl of Halifax, formerly Conservative Leader in the House of Lords, and intimate colleague of the Prime Minister. While recognizing and expressing sympathy for the Government, which he thought had found "it was extremely difficult . . . to maintain the simple direct line of their predecessors, which was to have no compromise in the matter at all," Lord Halifax thought the concession to the commercial advocates "profoundly wrong". Since the Government disliked introducing sponsored broadcasts they had been unable to satisfy backbenchers who wanted "free competition on commercial lines," but they had sought to draft a White Paper "which might be regarded as an innocuous compromise." As Chairman of the General Advisory Council of the BBC, Halifax was convinced that this action constituted "a landmark in the history of British broadcasting," and he was "profoundly sorry that it should be the Party with whom I have been associated who have made themselves responsible for it." Even beyond this, Lord Halifax warned the Government that had Lord Reith intended to divide the House on his motion, "I should feel obliged to vote with him."

Not until the sixth speaker, Lord Mancroft, did the Government hear words of commendation for its proposals, and even then they were told that they should have gone farther and faster and proposed sponsored radio as well. From his stress on the evil of monopoly to the copious citation of Sir Frederick Ogilvie's letter to *The Times* of June 26, 1946, which had been widely circulated by the Conservative backbench Group, Lord Mancroft might have been speaking from a brief prepared by the Broadcasting Group. He feared that the Government's hesitation might be utilized by the BBC to delay the introduction of commercial television; it seemed pertinent to him that the London Passenger Transport Board had put 1,230 buses on the streets since 1938 at a cost of £4,500 each, which was more than the cost of a Very High Frequency Station, without public criticism; and he attacked BBC expenditure on the Third Programme — "I even understand it now and again"—because only one per cent of the population listened to it. The only departure from the line of argument developed by the Broadcasting Group was Lord Mancroft's unstinting praise for the objectivity and political independence of the BBC.

As the spokesman for the Government, Lord De La Warr, Postmaster-General and nominally in charge of the Cabinet's programme, resented most strongly the "unproven assertion . . . by speaker after speaker" that the White Paper represented "a scuttling of the BBC." On the contrary, the Postmaster-General insisted that the Government agreed that the BBC had "given the United Kingdom a broadcasting system that is the envy of many other countries. . . . We have here a system and an organization that has justified itself in practice. . . ." He also recognized "that our national future, in terms of our thoughts, feelings and standards of values, is at stake." It was a difficult subject producing strong and divided views, which explained why the Government had required six months to formulate a policy and why it was, inevitably, a compromise proposal. Speaking for himself, Lord De La Warr thought it was a "conflict of negatives . . . it is really a case of deciding whether our dislike of monopoly is stronger or weaker than our dislike of sponsored or commercial broadcasting." Certainly it was not shyness that had dictated omitting "commercial" from the Paper, for "it is clear that under our proposals commercial television is possible, but it is equally true that there are other possible ways of providing competition." Public bodies including universities were other potential competitors of the BBC, but because "it seemed to us such a long way away" no mention was made of this alternative in the Paper. Though it was thought that commercial television was a likely interpretation of the White Paper's phrasing, it certainly did "not exclude some other method of bringing about that competition. It was for that reason that the word 'commercial' was quite deliberately left out, and not because we were either shy or coy about its use." The Government sought to offer an alternative to the principle of monopoly while preserving the integrity of the BBC, thereby avoiding making the public solely dependent on sponsored television. In any case the Postmaster-General was certain that the British people would not respond favourably to "the same vulgarities and horrors, and even tiresomeness, which are apparently so popular elsewhere." Sound broadcasting was not to be altered because "there are the three separate national programmes and a good many local variations."* As additional assurance to those concerned for the BBC, Lord De La Warr reiterated the Government's intention to see that "competition against the BBC will not start until that organization is at least well on the way to supplying the whole country. . . . This means building five new low-powered television stations which, with the existing stations, would give service to something in the neighbourhood of 90 per cent of the population." Engineers estimated that this would take two years from the starting date. Finally, he emphasized that broadcasting was not a Party issue, and "the day the BBC becomes a matter of Party controversy will be a bad day, not only for the BBC, but for the country as a whole." This position was to be forfeited as the struggle within the Conservative Parliamentary Party became more bitter and the

* The *Manchester Guardian* had thought that "the omission of any reference to sound broadcasting suggests that advertisers and manufacturers may be less interested in this field." Editorial, "Broadcasting", May 16, 1952.

public phase of the controversy confronted the Government with the possibility of a humiliating defeat.

Lord Elton, at this time the only member of the House of Lords who had served on the Ullswater Committee which in 1934 conducted the first official investigation of the BBC, went on record "as quite convinced that the introduction of commercialized sponsored broadcasting would be a disaster. . . ." However he did think there was a good deal to be learned from American methods, in particular "the fact that it does keep a number of highly talented men and women broadcasting fairly continuously."

Viscount Hailsham, whose passionate denunciation of commercial broadcasting was ultimately to become an advantage to the proponents, excoriated the leaders of his Party for what he considered to be the inconsistency of the White Paper. Though he had "intended to deliver a diatribe against" the proposals, he had come to realize "that what I had attributed to vice must be ascribed to a pardonable ignorance." The inconsistency which he deplored was that of opening the Paper with an encomium of the BBC and then advocating the introduction of a commercial system. He considered that the argument over monopoly or private enterprise in broadcasting was meaningless, or irrelevant, for wider choice depended on the number of channels available and not on the method of finance selected. Commercial broadcasting was to be condemned in his judgment because it distorted the purpose of broadcasting "by reason of the fundamental purpose for which the vehicle is used—not broadcasting for its sake but its use as a medium in which advertisements can live." He considered that the introduction of sponsored television was "an attempt, possibly deliberate and possibly misguided, to kill the BBC in the end, to impose upon it sentence of death but to allow a stay of execution. . . . The idea is to wreck the life's work of the noble Lord [Reith] by gradual means. It is hoped that the BBC will continue as a monopoly with sound broadcasting but that as television develops, with its new sponsored broadcasting and competitive techniques, it will come to take the place of the monopoly more and more." If the Government had wanted to experiment with commercial broadcasting they could have done so by permitting the Corporation "to allow sponsoring on limited terms and for limited periods," rather than proposing to erect new stations "consecrated to the principle which is so gravely in doubt." Though out of favour with the Party leadership* at this time, and denied a place in the Churchill Government, Viscount Hailsham was a dedicated Conservative and he was concerned for the political fortunes of his Party. Because of the balance existing between the two major parties, he was alarmed at "the numerous signs I have seen which seem to indicate that the Government are almost going out of their way to antagonize moderate opinion outside the Conservative Party merely to gratify the somewhat confused political pressures from within."

In the final half-hour of the first day's debate, the Government received support for its commercial proposal from three self-declared spokesmen for "the younger generation," Lord Foley, the Earl of Buckinghamshire, and Lord Montagu of Beaulieu. As Lord Montagu put it: "We are the new generation of radio listeners, and we are the people for whom this legislation is ultimately intended."† To a considerable extent they did represent and speak for the new generation of Conservatives. Their attitude conflicted sharply with the kind of responsibility expressed by the Earl of Halifax, Viscount Hailsham, Lord Brand and others of all parties who believed that broadcasting should be a public

* In this debate he was rebuked by the Lord Chancellor, Lord Simonds, who suggested that if Lord Hailsham had the sole right of speaking in the House of Lords "it might not be a valuable one, for he would soon find himself speaking to the empty air."

† The Broadcasting Group made much of their claim that the average age of those who favoured commercial broadcasting was more than ten years younger than the supporters of the BBC.

service seeking to preserve standards and values, and to raise the public taste, not merely to reflect it. In contrast to this concern for leadership in standards and ethics, Lord Foley, who had declared his enthusiasm for sponsored broadcasting in the 1946 debate, favoured elimination of the Third Programme so that its wave-length could be made available for commercial broadcasting. He saw no difficulty in determining what was worthwhile. "After all, the success of a play or a film can easily be judged by noting the number of people in the theatre. If the theatre is full, you know immediately that the play is a success; if the house is empty you know it is not." Similarly, the fact that Radio Luxembourg claimed "an average listening figure of over 6,000,000 people" convinced Lord Foley and the Earl of Buckinghamshire "that the great mass of the British listening public is in favour of commercial broadcasting. . . ." He also liked the "friendliness and lack of formality" characteristic of Radio Luxembourg programmes in contrast to "the often rather cold-blooded approach of the BBC." Lord Montagu also noted that the British Forces in Germany were "listening more and more to the American Forces Network, to which they grew accustomed during the war and which they now prefer to the BBC."

When the debate resumed on Monday, May 26th, Lord Macdonald of Gwaenysgor, Paymaster-General in the Labour Government, posed what many considered to be the fundamental objection to sponsored broadcasting. "Is it wise," he asked, "for this country to follow up the craze that we find growing rapidly in some countries to commercialize everything? Is it really wise? Will it add to the dignity of this great country of ours? Surely there are some things which are too sacred to be commercialized. Nothing gives me more satisfaction as a Briton than that we in this country have not trod that path very far. The main reason why I am against sponsored broadcasting is that I am afraid that it is a step in the direction of commercialization."

In direct contrast, Lord Brabazon of Tara, speaking as "an unrepentant pro-sponsorite," restated much of the argument he had presented in the 1946 debate on the Labour Government's White Paper. He explained Lord Reith's objections on the ground that "nobody likes to see his child mutilated and emasculated; and that is the proposal which sponsoring brings in summarily to the BBC." To get immediate action for this emasculation, Lord Brabazon proposed that sponsored television be given the use of BBC facilities between 6 p.m. and 8 p.m., during which time there were as yet no BBC television programmes.

Although a member of the General Advisory Council of the BBC, Lord Brand opposed the Government's proposals, not for that reason, "but because I have listened to commercial broadcasting for nearly six years. The result of that experience is that I heartily dislike it, for many reasons, and regard our system as incomparably better." Perhaps, he suggested, British advertising would not be quite the same as American, less vigorous and less humorous, "but essentially advertising is the same everywhere: every advertiser does everything that he thinks is best needed to sell his product." With Lord Macdonald he had a moral reason for objecting to commercial broadcasting, since it spreads "the idea that everything is for sale." Lord Brand recognized that the debate centred on the real question: "Must we give the people exactly what they want, or what they are supposed to want? . . . Are the public always to be flattered and followed, as they certainly will be, if we give way to advertising? Or do the community try to use this great instrument, not only for entertainment, but also for enlightenment? If so, we shall reject on principle any commercial advertising."

Lord Hawke declared his intention to speak because over the week-end the Press had given what he believed to be the erroneous impression "that your Lordships' House" was opposed to commercial television. Unlike several of the opposition speakers, Lord Hawke was certain that "the conscience of the British public is such that they will never stand for any form of sponsored broadcast which is not in good taste." True, "of course everything cannot be of the highest possible standard," just as some of the BBC programmes are drivel, but "at least I am perfectly certain that what is given will be drivel in good taste—if indeed it be drivel." In any case, he estimated that were the British public asked if they would like an additional programme for which they were not going to pay at all, "they would say every time: 'We will have something for nothing'."

A former BBC Governor, Lord Kenswood, in replying to Lord Brabazon, posed another of the differences that was to continue to separate those opposed to commercial broadcasting from its proponents. He thought that the argument was not really over competition for the BBC, but rather a drive to extend the hours of broadcasting. It was his opinion "that television already absorbs as many hours of the day as is good for us. In fact, I should like to reduce the hours. But to increase them I think is a crime against the health of the people of this country." Lord Llewellin, who had served on the General Advisory Council of the BBC for five years, seized on this point to suggest that the BBC had actually resisted the development of television. In his opinion it was up to the parents to decide the amount of time children should spend looking at television. For this reason he joined with "the younger and more adventurous Peers" in supporting the Government.

Suggesting that these so-called "adventurous young" Peers were "taking adventures at other people's expense, rather than their own," Lord Radcliffe thought the proposal for commercial television "too dangerous a hazard for the Government to wish to go forward with it." He noted that it was not the wise and mature, but the young people that face the "danger of a cheapening of tone, of the touch that makes all things common." What kind of competition was being proposed? "Competition in trying to give to the public of this country the best service of information, of education, of art and culture that a service can provide; or competition in the meaner art of trying, by all decent means, to seduce and attract the largest circle of customers that you can win?" Lord Radcliffe warned that "it is the level of culture of this country that you are needlessly putting to the hazard" and he did not believe this should be "put up for sale over any shop counter."

None of this argument impressed Lord Gifford because "the elder statesmen of this House" didn't understand entertainment, "and, after all, the main object of broadcasting is to give entertainment and recreation to the people." He doubted that Lord Halifax or Lord Brand were regular followers of "Mrs. Dale's Diary" (a popular radio serial of a middle class family), or were qualified to rate the merits of dance bands.

In summing up for the Government the Lord Chancellor, Lord Simonds, insisted that the position of the BBC was to remain unaltered, "but the door is kept open for sponsored television." He seemed to imply that the Government's intentions were somewhat more tentative than some of its supporters indicated or desired. "The BBC will go on and there *may* . . . be sponsored television also." In addition he said, "it cannot but be *several years* before any licences can be granted" for commercial stations.* Apart from a scathing reference to Lord Hailsham, it was a moderate though not a conciliatory speech, perhaps reflecting the Government's embarrassment at the calibre of those Conservative Members who had denounced the White Paper proposal and a plea for their understanding of the Government's dilemma. "A great body of men, many of whom have spoken today, and whose opinion we respect, say one thing. On the other hand, we find a great body of people who take a diametrically opposite view. On each side there is an assertion of a moral principle. When you find such a thing as that, is it not wise statesman-

* Emphasis added. H.H.W.

ship to go by stages?" He was disturbed by the fervour with which some of the opponents had stressed a moral principle and suggested that they should remember Cromwell's admonition: "I beseech you, in the bowels of Christ, think that ye may be mistaken." In the end, Lord Simonds underscored the Government's determination to introduce commercial television and end the BBC's monopoly. He personally hoped "that in time it will lead to sponsored radio," for "the time has now come for the [BBC] monopoly, like all other monopolies, to come to an end."

The Government could have obtained no satisfaction from the debate, even though no division occurred because Lord Reith withdrew the motion. Of the twenty-nine speeches, seventeen were in opposition to the Government's proposal to introduce commercial television and, apart from two Cabinet spokesmen, ten supported the plan. More important than numbers, of course, was the fact that the opposition speakers included some of the most prominent Conservative figures—the Earl of Halifax, Lord Brand, Viscount Waverley, a respected independent like Lord Radcliffe, and the Liberal statesman Viscount Samuel. Though much was made of the fact that those critical of the Paper included several peers who were or had been closely associated with the BBC—an ex-Director-General, an ex-Governor, and six members of the General Advisory Council—the fact remained that no individuals of comparable stature could be found to defend the Government's policy.*

Failing to win the approval of those "whose opinion we

* Lord Brabazon had commented that a meeting of the Advisory Council of the BBC had been held on Wednesday, May 21, 1952, the eve of the debate, "when they were addressed by the Chairman, Lord Simon of Wythenshawe and by the Director-General, Sir William Haley—I suppose that was a sort of 'pep talk' for the debate. At all events it brought forth some formidable speeches in this House. The whole team has rallied round. . . . I must congratulate them on the noble work they are doing for monopoly."

respect," the Government had as well further antagonized the members of the Broadcasting Group. On May 28, 1952, in preparation for the debate on the White Paper in the House of Commons, the Group sent to Assistant Postmaster-General Captain David Gammans a very critical analysis of the Government's proposals. The White Paper was attacked generally for providing too many loopholes and too many opportunities for the BBC and the Post Office to prevent or indefinitely delay the introduction of commercial competition. They thought it sinister that paragraph 11 stated:

"The Government consider that the BBC have a continuing obligation to provide adequate national broadcasting services throughout the United Kingdom, and the fulfilment of this policy must clearly have first claim when labour and materials become available."

And the Group was especially incensed by the Postmaster-General's reiteration of this principle during the Lords' debate. "This means," Lord De La Warr had said, "building five new low-powered television stations which, with the existing stations, would give service to something in the neighbourhood of 90 per cent of the population." This would, they charged, enable the BBC to sabotage the development of commercial broadcasting by claiming that national coverage had not yet been attained.

They rejected the argument that Government limitations on capital investment explained the failure of the BBC to expand its television coverage or to develop Very High Frequency broadcasting. The commercial proponents insisted that the BBC had deliberately delayed these developments. Instead of using its capital construction money for these purposes the BBC, it was charged, had expended it on building transmitters for the Third Programme. These critics believed that Very High Frequency had not been pushed because it would have eliminated the wave-length shortage as a primary technical justification for the BBC monopoly. Now the backbenchers felt that the Government was ignoring the Beveridge Committee recommendation, as well as Selwyn Lloyd's minority report, that "development of Very High Frequency broadcasting should be regarded as important and urgent." Furthermore they charged, the Government had apparently accepted the BBC's estimate that the cost of establishing VHF and television stations was very great. It would have been more realistic, in their judgment, to have relied on cost figures from the radio industry, rather than from the BBC or the Post Office.

The White Paper had stated that a controlling body would have to be established "to introduce safeguards against possible abuses" in the proposed new system, and the Postmaster-General would grant licences on the advice of this body. It would not have authority over the BBC. In opposition to this, the Broadcasting Group was insistent that there be established a Broadcasting Commission, modelled after the FCC, which would control the BBC as well as the new system, allocate frequencies, control the capital construction programme and recommend the licensing of new stations. They based this demand on a Conservative Party pamphlet, "Britain Strong and Free," which had proposed that public and private road transport should be controlled by the same licensing authorities. It was argued that such a Commission would serve to insulate the control of broadcasting from politics, but it also reflected a general suspicion that the civil servants in the Post Office favoured the continuation of the BBC's monopoly.[2]

Though the Conservative backbenchers appreciated Captain Gammans' difficult position, since he was expected to support the Cabinet's proposal in the House of Commons, they urged him to modify the Government's declaration by saying in answer to backbench questions that commercial stations would be approved after *permission* to build the five small stations had been granted the BBC. The Group had the assurance of equipment manufacturers that once authorized the commercial stations would be completed within a matter of months. This time factor was a crucial issue for the proponents since they were determined to get a commercial system operating at least six months in advance of the next General Election.

On Wednesday, June 11, 1952, in the House of Commons, Sir David Maxwell Fyfe, Home Secretary, moved approval of the Government's proposals for the future of the BBC.[3] Noting that it was almost three years since the Beveridge Committee was created and "there is no subject which has had so much previous discussion," Sir David felt certain "there cannot now be any complaint that these problems have not been well and truly ventilated." The Government had recognized the need for a careful consideration of the issues and for that reason had first extended the Charter and Licence of the BBC for six months. Now the new documents had to be approved to come into effect by July 1, 1952. In recommending a ten-year Charter rather than accepting the Beveridge recommendation of an unlimited period, or the Labour Government's proposed fifteen-year Charter, the Government had taken account of the possibility of extensive technical developments, especially in Very High Frequency broadcasting. Progress in this field could conceivably, they thought, change the whole basis of sound and television for Great Britain. They appreciated the momentous nature of the decision to alter the future pattern of broadcasting control, since in its twenty-six years the BBC had "built up, both in peace and war, a reputation which is unsurpassed and, I think," said Sir David, "unequalled in any other country." Nevertheless, "the Government do not propose to ask Parliament to commit itself to continuation throughout the next ten years of the BBC's exclusive privilege of broadcasting. . . ." It was apparent that the Government were still seeking to reconcile opponents of the change while keeping their own backbench critics pacified. To this end Sir David's presentation gave the impression of reasonableness,

courtesy to those raising questions, and a quiet toler-
ance for differences of opinion. He stressed that the BBC
would be maintained intact and that "we intend that the
BBC shall be allotted the resources to *complete* its programme
of lower-power television stations and to make *reasonable
progress* with the introduction of High Frequency sound broadcasting *before* any competitor is admitted to a share of the
national resources." Just as in the Lords' debate, there was
created a sense of the indefinite timing of the change—
"when circumstances make it feasible . . . no one can postu-
late when that will be. . . ."* Similarly, it was apparent in
the Home Secretary's presentation that at this stage the
Government had not formulated any organization for the
new system. There was a definite commitment that the
competitors would have to rely on "advertisements and
sponsored programmes for their income," since only the
BBC would receive licence revenue. This would not mean
Americanization or debasement of broadcasting standards,
assured Sir David, because "we have our typically British
way of resolving problems of taste, just like any other
problem. We are a much more mature and sophisticated
people. Is it really to be suggested that such a people as ours
are unfit to decide what they want to see? . . . Are they unfit
for anything but the Governess state?" To those who
wondered why commercial competition was not to be permitted in sound, Sir David observed that "as a medium for
advertising, television offers certain advantages over the
sound programmes. It may prove to be the way in which
sponsoring can earn its revenue and acclimatise itself to
British taste, which is quite different from American taste,
in a field where British taste is still in a formative stage."

For the Opposition Mr. Herbert Morrison introduced a

* Even Herbert Morrison believed that the actual introduction
of commercial television was remote. "I admit," he said, "they are
not immediately committing this House, but they are committing
us to the principle of the thing. . . ." H.C. Debs. 502:250.

counter motion regretting the decision of the Government to introduce commercial television and the change in the method of appointing the Governors. He thought it curious that the White Paper had not mentioned sponsored television and he thought it likely in view of the Lord Chancellor's statement in the House of Lords' debate, and despite the Home Secretary's denial, that sound radio would also be commercialized. Much of his criticism focused on the debasement of standards under commercial television since he thought that "the very nature of the thing is that it must be a chase for listeners and viewers." He quoted extensively from a *Time* magazine account of a report to the FCC on the amount of violence depicted on American television screens.[4] Since the American advertising agencies in England would participate in the new commercial development "we may get that very Americanism about which the Home Secretary seemed to be apprehensive." It was also evident that Mr. Morrison thought it was possible to have too much television, an attitude shared by many of the opponents, and he was opposed to the high incomes paid for commercial broadcasting performers. Not only would this produce difficulty for the BBC, but "I am not sure that these vast incomes for that limited amount of work is a good thing." He tried to convince the Government that "there is a grave public disquiet" about their scheme and that "they have not got public opinion with them on this point. . . ." And with real Establishment flavour, Mr. Morrison warned the Government that the opponents of commercial television spoke for Britain. "I believe with absolute sincerity . . . that this proposed development is totally against the British temperament, the British way of life and the best or even reasonably good British traditions."

Captain Charles Waterhouse, in replying to Mr. Morrison, admitted that there "may not seem to be a public demand" for commercial broadcasting, but this he explained by the silence of the Press, the relative absence of discussion of the issue on the BBC, and the fact that it had not been debated before in the Commons. He did not believe that standards would decline because "people will judge of the best and will switch on to the best." Captain Waterhouse was disappointed that the Government did not open up sound radio for advertising, but he was "more than a little shaken" that Sir David Maxwell Fyfe's opening speech should imply that the change would be in "the very remote future. If he really means that— I hope he does not—then I think he was not being completely sincere to the House on the terms of the White Paper."

Mr. Malcolm Macpherson, Labour M.P. from Stirling and Falkirk and a former teacher, opposed the Government on a point one might have anticipated from a Conservative. On the argument of "giving the people what they want" Mr. Macpherson suggested that it is not a proper function of the House to deny a policy thought to be wise because it would not win approval in a plebiscite. He thought one of the important things about British Government was that "the people expect their representatives to be a little wiser in political matters and a little more specially concerned with policy than they are. . . ." The real issue, as he saw it, was "not primarily the standard of the programmes but the standard of our national life which will undoubtedly become debased if we increase the number of agencies by which money power can affect it."

Sir Ian Fraser, a former BBC Governor, had changed his views since the 1946 debate and was now working closely with the backbench Broadcasting Group. Though he had testified before the Beveridge Committee[5] only that consideration should be given to using sponsored programmes on television and Overseas Broadcasting, Sir Ian now favoured ending the BBC's monopoly in both sound and television. In direct conflict with what seemed to have been his earlier interpretation, he held that the Crawford Committee had gone along with the technicians' recommendation for monopoly because "very few of us knew anything about the technicalities of broadcasting and therefore the technical men were able to put forward their views without being called to account or criticized."[6] He was not satisfied with Sir David Maxwell Fyfe's accepting the necessity for delay, insisting that a competing system could start at once with currently unused BBC facilities. Certainly, "the Government must make a better statement at the end of the debate than they have made at the beginning about the priority of the BBC. . . . If all priorities and absolute priorities are to go to the BBC for a long period of time," Sir Ian warned, "we shall not see this change which the Government say is a proper one to make. I, for one, will support the Government, but I hope they will give us some assurance that it will not be too long before they give us this greater freedom on the air."

Only one Conservative Member, Mr. Beverley Baxter, actually attacked the Government, and he made it plain that but for the imposition of a three-line Whip by the Government he would have voted with the Opposition. He would rather have sponsored television than a socialist government so "I shall vote with a heavy heart simply because I do not want this Government out." Apart from his close association with Lord Beaverbrook and the *Daily Express*, which was now violently opposed to commercial television, Baxter's opposition reflected his experience in the United States where he had found that sponsored programmes meant exposure to the "terrorization of the mass suggestion of advertising."

Mr. Charles Orr-Ewing spoke briefly to refute the allegation of Mr. (now Lord) Shackleton that those pressuring for this change in the pattern of broadcasting had a "vested interest in sponsored radio." Though at this time a director of A. C. Cossor, Ltd., radio and television manufacturers, Mr. Orr-Ewing explained that "we are doing this, not because of any monetary gain, but because we have fought ever since 1945 in our constituencies on the theme of trust the people—set the people free to choose their own programmes." Mr. Ian Harvey, a director of the advertising firm of W. S. Crawford, Ltd., made a similar point during the Licence debate on June 23rd, explaining that actually "this desire for sponsorship" would cost him money. For, "if one studies the promotion of advertising for radio or television in this country, one will realize at once that it will require new resources, new equipment, and new staff and it will, in fact, give the advertising agent less remuneration than the use of the normal methods of advertising."[7]

The major statement for the Broadcasting Group was made by its chairman, Mr. John Profumo, who denied that he had interests in advertising, radio or any other industry. He was extremely blunt in criticizing the White Paper for not being explicit. "I do not like mere indications. I should have liked to see it come out flatly in favour of breaking the BBC monopoly, not only in vision but in sound broadcasting." The backbenchers were "greatly perturbed by a declaration of policy which, at first sight, can be read in two ways." However, they would support the Government on three assumptions: first, that the Government intended to allow "competitive television stations" to start operating "at the earliest possible time"; secondly, that there would be no delay in giving the radio manufacturers the necessary technical information so they could start manufacturing sets capable of receiving the new stations; and, thirdly, that a control body would soon start working out the standards to be followed by the new companies. Commenting on those who were supporting the continuation of the BBC, Mr. Profumo considered their motives to be self-evident. The Labour Party opposition was traceable to socialist dislike for competition, and the Press simply feared the loss of advertising revenue. The officials of the BBC, "a very mighty host" including the Governors and members of the advisory councils, wanted no change in its status and these "guardians" were "almost powerful enough to be able to intimidate the Government." Then there were the intellectuals, "who raise their hand and voice in horror in case Mr. and Mrs. John Citizen should possibly become culturally corrupted by entertainment assuming priority over social purpose in broadcasting." Though Mr. Profumo greatly admired the intellectuals, he thought it imperative that it be remembered "we are not a nation of intellectuals" and the average listeners, for whom he was speaking, deserved "the best possible entertainment which can be given to them."

The Assistant Postmaster-General, Captain David Gammans, in closing the debate for the Government, went a long way towards meeting the Broadcasting Group's request that he modify the Government's commitment to allow the BBC to complete its coverage before any competing stations were authorized. "Several of my hon. friends," he said, "have raised the point as to whether the Government are in earnest, and I want to make this quite clear. The Government are in earnest, not only over breaking the BBC monopoly, but also in permitting sponsored television." Furthermore, even though they had decided to give the BBC priority to complete building programmes which had been delayed because of capital restrictions, this did not mean that "competitive television must wait until the BBC extension is complete in all respects."

With the Government enforcing a three-line Whip the division was a foregone conclusion. The Opposition motion put by Mr. Morrison was rejected by a vote of 304 to 276, and the main question with which Sir David Maxwell Fyfe had introduced the debate was carried by 297 votes to 269. Two days later the Government laid before the House the new Licence and Agreement which, with the Charter,* would provide the legal framework for the BBC until 1962. It was apparent that the Government would have no difficulty in mustering the necessary votes,† so the Licence debate on

* The Charter is given under Royal prerogative and does not require Commons' approval.

† The Licence and Agreement was approved by 302 votes to 267.

June 23rd was something of an anti-climax. Its principal
interest was Mr. Patrick Gordon Walker's unsuccessful
attempt to extract from the Government its timing for the
introduction of the new system. He noted that the Lord
Chancellor had said it would be "several years," while in
Commons the Assistant Postmaster-General had stressed that
commercial broadcasting would begin "before long". Mr.
Gordon-Walker was sure that the Government could not
implement its declared policy for "several years" and he
warned the newly formed Associated Broadcasting Development Company that a Labour Government would "certainly
not carry on the policy implied in this non-exclusive Licence."

The announcement, on June 20, 1952, of the formation of
this private company was made in an effort to convince the
Government that its commitment to "introduce some element
of competition" was taken seriously and to demonstrate the
fact that powerful financial and manufacturing interests were
prepared to invest money in the new broadcasting scheme.*

* Although the announcement was made in June, the actual
formation of the Associated Broadcasting Development Company
did not take place until August 7, 1952.

CHAPTER VI

A SOUFFLÉ OF INTERESTS

FOR ACHIEVING THE Government's initial commitment to competitive television the evidence would seem to support the contention of Mr. John Rodgers, M.P., that major credit is due to the "five or six Conservative backbenchers who worked day and night on the project."* Credit is due also to their devoted allies in the Cabinet, the Whips' Office and the Conservative Party headquarters. Nevertheless, despite skilful manipulation of the ideological issue of monopoly, the undeniable existence of latent hostility to the BBC, and the resentment of the "new Conservatives" for the Party's elder statesmen, in combination with the economic difficulties of the Churchill Government, it is still not clear how so small a group was able to make its influence decisive. Even conceding that all these disciples of commercial television were "persuasive advocates and persons of considerable charm,"[1] it would strain credulity to believe that, working alone, they were able not only to wring the initial

* This evaluation is supported not only by those in Parliament, but also by the recollections of Mr. Michael Patmore, a director of J. Walter Thompson, Ltd., by Mr. Norman Collins of Associated Broadcasting Company who worked very closely with the Conservative committee, and by Mr. Cyrus Ducker, at the time a director of London Press Exchange, who collaborated with the backbenchers over a period of several years.

E   129

commitment from a reluctant Government, but could wage an ultimately successful campaign for two more years in the face of mounting and increasingly well-organized opposition. Why did the Government capitulate to the demands of this group? What were the interests working behind this group, providing support and intensifying the pressure, public and political, in the campaign for commercial broadcasting?

Perhaps in suggesting answers, however partial, to these questions in this particular instance, insight may be gained into how pressure from economic interests operates under the conditions set by the British Constitution. For despite repeated disclaimers to the contrary by proponents of commercial television,* it soon becomes clear that not only were "powerful financial and manufacturing interests . . . prepared to invest money in the new broadcasting scheme," but they had been and were continuing to work for its introduction. The study of how these interests operated reveals the limitations imposed by looking merely at the formal structure of a political party, or of government. Certainly in this instance it becomes impossible to draw a line of demarcation between the advertising agencies, or the radio and television manufacturers, or financial groups, and the Conservative Party. For actual operating purposes the Party organization became a vast network of interests which, as Professor Finer observed, were "not affiliated but aligned" with the Party.[2] In this particular operation the specific

---

* For example, on June 22, 1954, Captain L. P. S. Orr, in addition to disclaiming any personal financial interest, stated that "Any suggestion that the bill was fostered by commercial interests is a complete figment of the imagination of the Party opposite. I know of no warranty for it." (H.C. Debs. 529:327.) And Lord De La Warr told the Advertisers' Association: the television "scheme is sometimes represented as an advertisers' ramp. Never at any time had your association or its members pressed the Government on this subject." (*The Times*, June 30, 1954, and the Oldham *Evening Chronicle*, June 29, 1954.)

interests were intermingled not only with the Conservative Party but, to a considerable extent, with the Government itself. Thus one may ask, at what point were Members speaking as M.P.s representing their constituents, and when were they speaking as directors, managers, employees, of advertising agencies, market research organizations, or radio and television manufacturers? This is not to imply any improper, dishonest, or unethical conduct—unless one were to hypothecate philosopher-kings who have been freed from the commitments of ordinary men. In actuality, men go into politics, among other reasons, to further their recognized interests and their conception of the good life. That this tends inevitably to reflect their career interests is hardly a revelation. And given the nature and philosophies of the two major parties, it is inevitable that the Conservative Party, and not the Labour Party, should be meshed almost totally with the vast complex of commerce, business, and finance. This was one factor weakening the resistance of those Members who did not particularly like commercial broadcasting, for given their general orientation towards business they could hardly be expected to condemn on principle the reliance of broadcasting on advertising revenue. Pointing out that the Labour Party in turn does receive support from a few wealthy individuals and some business representatives is a diverting and even, on occasion, an amusing debating point that is completely irrelevant in analysing the resources of the two parties.

It is customary in describing lobbying tactics to focus attention on the formal associations of industry, commerce, labour or the professions, basing analysis of their activities on the authority of annual reports, or official association statements. In this drive for commercial television, although the Labour Opposition and the newspapers frequently referred in general terms to the pressure campaign of advertising agencies, advertisers, and radio equipment manufacturers, there was, in fact, no unanimity even within these groups.

One of the difficulties in presenting an account of this campaign is the complexity of the alliances and the contrast between formal trade association statements and informal operations. Thus, most observers assumed that the cinema producers, cinema operators, and theatre managers were united in opposition to the new television scheme. It is true that Associated British Pictures Corporation, Ltd. (ABC), campaigned actively and financially supported the National Television Council,* but J. Arthur Rank, Ltd., the other major producer, appears to have taken no action and never replied to a National Television Council plea for support. Interests originally opposed to commercial television, as for example, Granada Theatres, Ltd.,† ABC, and several newspapers, moved quickly to participate once it became apparent that it was to be introduced.‡ The Society of West End Theatre Managers was actively and directly involved in opposition, while its vice-president, Mr. Prince Littler, was busy forming one of the first television programme companies. At one point it was believed that Lord Beaverbrook was actively interested in participating in commercial

* This was the pressure group, formed in 1953, with the aim of preventing the introduction of commercial television. See Chapter VII for a discussion of its operations.

† Granada Theatres, Ltd., had told the Beveridge Committee "that the right of access to the domestic sound and television receivers of millions of people carries with it such great propaganda power that it cannot be entrusted to any persons or bodies other than a public corporation or a number of public corporations." (Beveridge Report, II, p. 540.)

‡ According to reports both these companies had been preparing for commercial television for some time. ABC made a first application for permission to stage programmes before the Independent Television Authority was formed, and "every year since the war [Sydney Bernstein] and his executives [of Granada] have spent several months in the United States studying television." (Evening Standard, August 26, 1954.)

television, only to change suddenly and, through the *Daily Express*, become one of its more vehement opponents.

In 1953 the official position of the Radio Industry Council was that the industry wanted alternative television programmes but it was not taking sides as to who should run them. Thus, Lord Burghley, speaking at the annual dinner of the Radio Industry Council, November 18, 1953, declared: "It is the view of the Industry that there should be more programmes, but it is not our job, here or in the Council, to say what method should be used." This attitude led Sir Robert Renwick, pro-commercial industrialist and City stockbroker, to accuse some manufacturers of "hardening of the intellectual arteries" in their approach to commercial broadcasting. "Why all this sitting on the fence? Why the attitude that it really hasn't got anything to do with you? I am amazed that in a young and great and virile industry such as yours there should in certain quarters be such hesitation and timidity in putting the competitive television knob on the set."[3] However, the Council had submitted to the Beveridge Committee a memorandum written for them by Mr. Charles Orr-Ewing, then with Cossor, Ltd., urging the adoption of sponsored television. In presenting this view the Council specifically warned that it could not "represent fully the views of every individual firm within our organization." Many, perhaps a majority, of equipment manufacturers regretted that the Council had supported commercial television before the Beveridge Committee. Mr. Jules Thorn, chairman and managing director of Thorn Electric Industries, Ltd., whose Ferguson Radio and TV Division was one of the largest manufacturers, is reported to have said, after three weeks in the United States watching commercial programmes, that he was a firm opponent of sponsored television.[4] Many of the equipment firms had long established relationships with the BBC and, in addition, they felt it would be extremely dangerous to introduce any system that might undermine the ability of the BBC to maintain standards.

In contrast, Mr. C. O. Stanley of Pye, Ltd., was a most aggressive proponent of commercial television. In his annual report for that Company in 1949 he expressed a strong demand for sponsored television:

"Our television programmes in this country are excellent for the state of development of the industry, but if we are to provide the sort of programmes that the public will demand it is quite unlikely that they can come from the existing BBC revenue. They can, however, come from sponsored broadcasting, and I deplore the whispering campaign that has started against this obvious solution. It is understandable that a large number of people may not like American sponsored programmes, but there is no reason to suppose that all sponsored programmes have to be to the American pattern, any more than it is necessary to give up wearing neckties because one dislikes the American variety."[5]

When commercial television became a public issue the advertising trade association declared an organizational policy of neutrality in the political struggle and rather vehemently denied that they had made any attempt to persuade the Government to permit a commercial outlet. Thus Mr. Herbert Oughton, President of the Institute of Incorporated Practioners in Advertising, wrote, in a letter to the *Manchester Guardian*, on June 22, 1953: "It has been strongly suggested in several recent statements that advertisers and their advertising agencies are pressing for commercial television in this country. What the organizations representing advertisers and advertising agencies have done is to prepare professionally for the proper use of commercial television if and when it is introduced." To this end the Institute, in collaboration with the Incorporated Society of British Advertisers, submitted to the Postmaster-General in April, 1953, a joint memorandum on commercial television with suggestions for the regulation of programmes.[6] This declared policy of neutrality had not always been adhered to rigidly by the IIPA, for in its testimony to the Beveridge Committee and in its 1946 pamphlet, "Broadcasting", the Institute made explicit its desire for commercial broadcasting.[7]

Throughout the 1930's and 1940's the advertising agencies and the Institute did lobby for commercial radio. Up until 1939 there was a real expectation that advertising would be given an opportunity to use one of the BBC channels. This hope of at least some of the agencies was apparently based on the growing popularity of the Continental broadcasts and an assumed lessening of public hostility to radio advertising. However, until 1952 they never expected to be given a broadcasting system independent of the BBC* The outbreak of war meant, of course, that all advertising was sharply curtailed, but not all efforts to obtain commercial radio outlets.† Interest in post-war commercial broadcasting was sustained by frequent discussions in the trade journals. The *Advertisers' Weekly*, on January 6, 1944, reported an official of J. Walter Thompson, Ltd., as saying that "if domestic enterprise fails to provide the means through the British Government or the BBC, our clients in Britain can be reached from America, whether the authorities like it or

* Not all agencies would have been satisfied with use of a BBC channel. "Although there may be a majority . . . who feel that the BBC should father sponsored radio in this country, it is by no means certain that a majority of radio listeners would concur." The difficulty was that the BBC must maintain standards and "those standards might not be convenient for advertisers." (*Advertisers' Weekly*, November 15, 1945.)

† Barry Wells, in *Sound Wave Illustrated*, June, 1946, wrote: "At no time during the war have those advertising agents (J. Walter Thompson, Crawford) let up in their radio activities. Plans have been discussed, ideas burnished up, any flagging enthusiasm has been whipped up again. Lately these activities have increased."

not."* In the same issue of the *Weekly* a national advertiser is quoted: "While we would prefer our money to go to a British concern, and our programme to be transmitted on British soil, it is only a sentimental or patriotic viewpoint. If the Americans provide something first or better or more equitable with regard to charges, they will get the business." The Managing Director of Carter's Pills also emphasized this point: "If we do not get a service from the BBC in years to come, we are going to make our own arrangements for radio advertising."[8]

During and after the war there were frequent accounts in the trade papers and the popular Press of technical developments which would make it possible to cover the British Isles with commercial broadcasts from the Continent or Eire, from ships anchored offshore, or even from the United States. There were rumours that Radio Luxembourg or Radio Andorra were to be taken over by American broadcasting companies and American advertising agencies. However speculative and whatever their origin, these dramatic stories perhaps served to keep the issue alive.†

* When Mr. Christopher Mayhew, writing in *The Observer*, referred to this statement, Mr. Douglas Saunders of J. Walter Thompson objected that this was "as mischievous as it is untrue," but he did not deny that the statement had been made. (*Observer*, June 21, 1953.)

† For examples see *John Bull*, June 1, 1946, "Radio Pirates": "The BBC is threatened with commercial competition on an unprecedented scale. No less than seven corporations registered in the U.S. are believed to be planning broadcast services to this country from suitable Continental countries." *The People*, June 2, 1946: "A mystery representative of an American radio organization" has already tried to buy an Army station in Reykjavik and three Danish-owned ships to be used to broadcast to Britain; and *Cavalcade*, July 6, 1946, "Sponsored Invasion": ". . . huddles are now going on in New York, where it is recognized that the beaming of sponsored programmes towards Britain will be a big source of income in the near future."

With the Labour Government completely unsympathetic
to advertising and the agency leadership united in antipathy
to the Labour Government, efforts to persuade that Government to make concessions were deemed futile. What was
probably a common reaction in advertising circles to a
Labour victory was expressed by *Advertisers' Weekly*:
"Supporters of sponsored radio will be the first to suffer a
set-back to their plans. It is extremely unlikely that a Socialist
majority in the House will support any proposal for a radical
change in the BBC . . ."[9]

The increasing public caution of the IIPA reflected several
factors. One was certainly a conviction that the Labour Party
was an implacable foe, quite capable of introducing a tax on
advertising.* The resultant sensitivity to criticism from any
source was compounded by the genuine fear that were
organized advertising to be openly committed to lobbying
for commercial television it inevitably would bring general
condemnation. An editorial in *Advertisers' Weekly* had
warned that "any attempt prematurely to foist commercial
broadcasting on an antipathetic public might react unfavour-
ably on the sponsors, and also on the advertising business.
It would certainly stimulate that hostility to advertising so
often reflected in Parliamentary debates."[10]

This fear of arousing public hostility continued even under
the Conservative Government. At a week-end conference of
the Advertising Clubs of Great Britain in October, 1953,
Mr. E. J. Robertson, President of the Advertising Association, warned that the industry must take the initiative in
improving its standing. For "we have seen arise out of the
question of sponsored television the dormant hate of those
who think advertising people do not qualify to live in a
civilized community."[11] And the annual report of the
advertising and publishing trades section of the Manchester

* In his budget speech of November 12, 1947, Dr. Hugh Dalton
had actually proposed that only one half of advertising expenditure
should be considered allowable expense.

E*

Chamber of Commerce insisted that "throughout the whole controversy the advertising community as a whole has not yet expressed a desire that the alternative television programmes should be financed by advertising. . . ." The suggestion of advertising-financed programmes was merely "a logical outcome of American experience and purely a matter of national expediency." Therefore, the report concluded, "on these grounds, no case can be made out against the advertising business of wishing to 'foist' television advertising upon the public."[12]

The official neutrality of the Institute, like the Radio Industry Council, also stemmed from differences of opinion existing among agency personnel. A majority of the British agencies had no experience with broadcasting and were somewhat hostile just because it was unfamiliar. One advertising executive who was most active in the campaign for commercial television estimated that right up to the end, a vote of the Institute's membership would have been four to one in opposition to commercial television. This, he argued, was because on a numerical basis the small agencies had a majority of the members. *Advertisers' Weekly*, on September 17, 1953, reported that a poll of fifty agents showed 52 per cent personally favoured commercial television, 44 per cent were personally opposed, and only 46 per cent thought it would benefit advertisers as a whole. Many of the agencies had strong ties with newspapers and other media that were fearful that radio advertising would absorb the bulk of advertising expenditure and these agencies did not wish to risk antagonizing them. *

Some of the hostile agencies had accounts with large advertisers—Schweppes, Guinness, Cadbury, Watney Combe

* Mr. Leslie Pearl of Batten, Barton, Durstine & Osborne, Inc., in addressing the Advertising Creative Circle, reassured the Press that only "the marginal media on the fringe of usefulness of advertising" would be hurt financially by commercial television. (*Advertisers' Weekly*, July 2, 1953.)

Reid & Co., Hercules Cycle Co.—who were opposed to commercial broadcasting in Britain because of the increased cost of competitive advertising in a new media. Lord Moyne of Guinness pointed out that his company had done without advertising until 1928, when "we decided we must fall in line with others. None the less, I consider existing channels entirely adequate and commercial television an unnecessary and extravagant extension which the snowball effect of competition would oblige all advertisers to use if once it were opened."[13] A similar position was taken by Mr. S. H. Combe, chairman of Watney Combe Reid & Co., in his annual shareholders' report for 1953. He denied that the brewers would like to see commercial television introduced or that they had campaigned for it. "I consider that sufficient advertising channels already exist."[14]

Not a few agencies feared the capital investment that would be required, as well as the necessity for expanding agency personnel. Smaller agencies also thought they would be pushed out, unable to compete with the bigger firms. To some extent this reflected a general anti-American feeling, a reaction to the penetration by major New York firms. As one agency head wrote in a memorandum for Lord Hailsham's use in the House of Lords' debate on November 25, 1953, "from our own narrow point of view it is generally considered in the advertising profession that the introduction of commercial television is to the advantage of the very large agents, particularly those which are branches of big American agencies. This last class of firm has, as is well known, taken a prominent part in the agitation for commercial television, and no doubt hopes to tell advertisers that through their American connection they have the experience, facilities and know how in this new medium to a much more highly developed degree than the smaller or English agents." Those agencies and their clients who had used Continental radio stations before and after the war were most aggressive in demanding facilities in Britain. These included Erwin Wasey

who handled the Drene and Dreft account for Thomas
Hedley; J. Walter Thompson, Ltd., representing Lever
Brothers, Pal Persona Blades, Rowntree & Co., and Carter's
Little Liver Pills; and Masius & Ferguson with the Colgate-
Palmolive-Peet account. In general it was the larger British
agencies and the agencies with strong American connections
and experience that were the most enthusiastic advocates
of commercial television.

With the activities of the Institute somewhat muted because of this division of opinion among its membership, it
became necessary for proponents to work outside that body.
To this end, on the initiative of Mr. Cyrus Ducker, then a
director of the London Press Exchange, a private committee
of interested agency executives began meeting regularly in
the Board Room of S. H. Benson, Ltd., one of the biggest
British agencies. * The immediate impetus for this committee
apparently came from Mr. Ducker, who had returned from
the United States in 1948 with a keen realization of the
importance of commercial television and the conviction that
the British agencies could not permit advertising to be
legislated out of an opportunity to use this medium. He was
joined by Mr. Andrew Sinclair of J. Walter Thompson, Ltd.,
Mr. R. A. Bevan of S. H. Benson, Ltd., Mr. Vic Watson of
Erwin Wasey, Mr. Tom Morrison of Mather & Crowther
and, somewhat later, by Mr. Frank Dowling. After several
meetings it was decided to give this private committee a more
formal position. The Friday meetings were moved from the
Benson Board Room to the IIPA offices and, although the
Institute never formally renounced its official neutrality, the
informal group eventually became a subcommittee of the

* There is disagreement about the exact starting date of this
private committee. Mr. Drummond Armstrong recalled it as July,
1952, after the White Paper of May, 1952, with its commitment to
permit "some element of competition", Mr. R. A. Bevan placed it
as "early in 1953", and Mr. Ducker, whose records seemed most
complete, set it in 1948, after his return from the United States.

Committee on Radio, Cinema and Television of the Institute of Incorporated Practioners in Advertising.

In weekly meetings consideration was given to means for increasing the political support for commercial broadcasting and to devise the kind of advertising relationship that might be acceptable to the public, to advertisers, and to the Government. They were most concerned about the organization that was to be established and how the Postmaster-General would decide on those who were to receive licences. In a fluid situation in which the Government had reluctantly conceded something to backbench pressure but had not formulated precise policy it was inevitable that agents representing the bulk of advertising financial support for commercial television should exert considerable influence.

Many private meetings were held with the Postmaster-General, and especially with Captain Gammans, the Assistant Postmaster-General, and Sir Ben Barnett, the Post Office civil servant in charge of that Department's negotiations.* In their discussions they found that Lord De La Warr was always non-committal, though they felt that he never really liked the idea of introducing commercial television; but Captain Gammans was enthusiastic and Sir Ben Barnett was felt to be completely sympathetic to the advertising case. Mr. Drummond Armstrong, who was at the time Director of the IIPA and subsequently became a director of Colman, Prentis & Varley, recalls that a large part of their work with the Postmaster-General and other Ministers was educational. That is, these officials knew nothing about advertising and in particular they didn't at first grasp the difference between "sponsored programmes" and the more limited proposal advocated by the advertising committee.

Keenly aware of the formidable opposition to commercial broadcasting in any form, the advertising committee was concerned to prevent capture of the new set-up by more

* Barnett also served on the 1952 Television Advisory Committee.

extreme financial speculators and promoters. Their original hope was that the more responsible radio and television receiver manufacturers would take the lead and establish a television transmitter corporation similar to the original British Broadcasting Company. This proved to be impossible because Pye Radio, Ltd., and Electric & Musical Industries, Ltd., had already joined with others, in August, 1952, to form the Associated Broadcasting Development Company. Similarly a majority of the committee decided against advocating sponsored programmes on the American pattern, although many of the large American agencies and advertisers pushed for sponsoring right up to the end. It was felt by the others that this would be too sharp a break with British practice, as well as being too cumbersome, too expensive, and too demanding of agency personnel. In this sense the final Government bill was not a compromise since the committee obtained what it wanted. It is true that many restrictions were written into the bill, but these were accepted as necessary to get anything through and the agencies counted on a "sympathetic" administration of the act.

Reinforcing the efforts of the Conservative backbench "group" and interlocking with advertising agents and the Radio industry was a unique and powerful triumvirate: Mr. Norman Collins, Sir Robert Renwick, and Mr. C. O. Stanley. A crucial role was played by Mr. Collins who served as a persuasive advocate and public representative for their common interests. A successful popular novelist, Collins had joined the BBC Overseas Service in 1940, became head of the General Overseas Service five years later, served as Controller of the Light Programme in 1946, and as Controller of BBC Television from December 1, 1947, until October 13, 1950. Sir William Haley, then Director-General of the BBC, had concluded that Collins was not suitable for the newly created post of Director of Television, which also included a seat on the Board of Management. In the presence of Lord Simon, Chairman of the Board of Governors, Haley informed Collins, on October 13, 1950, that Mr. George Barnes, Director of the Spoken Word and Controller of the Third Programme, was to head the expanding television programme, but he hoped Collins would stay on as controller. As recollected by Lord Simon, Collins asked for two hours to think over his decision. "Like damned fools we agreed, with the result that Collins filled the afternoon papers with the story of his 'resignation' because the BBC wasn't interested in television."[15]

In his statement to the Press, Mr. Collins maintained that he resigned because of a "clash of principles. . . . The principle at stake is whether the new medium of television shall be allowed to develop at this, the most crucial stage of its existence, along its own lines and by its own methods, or whether it shall be merged into the colossus of sound broadcasting and be forced to adapt itself to the slower tempo and routine administration of the corporation as a whole." For three years he said he had sought "to conceal [from his television colleagues in the BBC] the apathy, disinterest and often open hostility towards the new medium which exists in some quarters of Broadcasting House."[16] Yet in September, 1949, at a luncheon of the Radio Industries Club, Collins had assured members that the BBC had been prepared to spend £12 million on capital development and expansion of television had Government policy permitted. Subsequently permission was granted to the BBC to spend as it chose "and I am glad to say that it chooses television."[17] And at the National Radio Exhibition in September, 1950, he had announced that the plans for the BBC's national television network were complete. However, Collins apparently felt that the appointment of Mr. Barnes meant that "a vested interest in sound broadcasting" would slow down the rate of television development "by efforts to adapt television in its diverse activities to the requirements of the older, simpler and fundamentally different medium of sound broadcasting."[18]

That this fear may have been warranted is suggested by

Lord Simon's observation that "perhaps four-fifths of the developments in the Broadcasting Corporation is in television; the Director-General presented the business to the Governors in such a way that they did not give more than one-fifth of their time to television, and no Governor had anything more than a very general knowledge of what was happening."[19] Lord Simon felt that it would have been desirable to appoint a subcommittee to keep the Governors informed of developments and difficulties in television expansion.

The official BBC explanation of Mr. Collins' departure was that he had been "a candidate for the post of Director of Television, and expressed himself as satisfied with its status and terms of appointment. He did not resign until he had been informed that he had not been appointed."[20] This action was to have impressive consequences for the future of the BBC and broadcasting in the British Isles. There is virtual unanimity among those most intimately involved that Collins' dedication, his intensive personal campaign to win support, and his energy, provided the vital element. A columnist in *The Observer* characterized him as ". . . the man who did more than any other single individual to bring commercial television to Britain."[21] Lord Simon actually insisted that "If we hadn't fired Collins there would be no commercial television now."[22] And Lord Bessborough commented that he and others active in the campaign "got cold feet" and wanted to drop out after they saw the formidable opposition to commercial television that developed, but Norman Collins and C. O. Stanley restored their morale and kept their feet to the fire.[23]

There certainly is no doubt of Collins' dedication to the cause. He was determined to break the BBC's monopoly, both in sound and television. Though political considerations dictated concentration first on television and avoiding a frontal assault on the existence of the Corporation, Collins personally intended to end the BBC's control over radio.

He ultimately formed a personal company for commercial radio broadcasting and declared that "if I have the time and energy, I shall take on this campaign, starting in 1961."[24]

In Collins' opinion his contribution was largely that of bringing the issue to the notice of the public. Until his resignation no one had been able to give full time to the commercial campaign—"I devoted three years of my life to it."[25] In addition, Collins was practically the only individual working for the commercial interests who combined extensive knowledge of television techniques and production with keenest enthusiasm for its entertainment potential. Others equally involved saw the development of television as an investment opportunity, as the most important advertising medium yet devised, or as expanding the market for television sets. With extensive experience in the actual use of television, Mr. Collins was persuasive in discussing the advantages of breaking the monopoly and avoiding bureaucratic control.

The proponents of commercial television felt that the Press was hostile, through fear of losing advertising revenue, and therefore reluctant to report the issues involved. Collins' resignation could not be ignored; it was widely reported and it served to launch his campaign most effectively with the charge that the BBC was hostile to television no matter how it was organized. He toured the country speaking to all kinds of groups and individuals, Rotary Clubs, educators, churchmen. A personable, extremely pleasant man, Collins was able to convince many that reliance upon advertising revenues need not result in vulgarization or in harm to the BBC. When the campaign against commercial television gained the support of bishops and university vice-chancellors, Collins approached many and persuaded some of them at least to soften their opposition. He recalls that the Church Assembly finally conceded that there was no moral objection to commercial television and advertising. Recognizing that one of the major obstacles was widespread hostility to the

"Americanization" of broadcasting he advocated the kind of compromise system that now exists and provided assurance that "excesses" of American television would be avoided, just as they had been in British newspapers, "by the exercise of our own national taste and feeling in the matter." In any case, Collins insisted, "no one advocates that this country should be given commercial radio and television on the American pattern."[26]

At least from the time of his resignation from the BBC in 1950, Collins was closely associated with Sir Robert Renwick and Mr. C. O. Stanley. They joined him in the creation of High Definition Films, Ltd., formed to manufacture electronic apparatus for making television films, and in founding the Associated Broadcasting Development Company, the first commercial television company to be formed. In both these ventures the three men worked with Lord Bessborough of the merchant banking firm of Robert Benson Lonsdale Co.

Renwick had extensive industrial interests, including fourteen directorships in the electrical industry. He had been Chairman of the County of London Electricity Supply Company, but resigned when it was nationalized, presumably because of his hostility to government ownership. Subsequently he became a partner in the City stockholding firm of W. Greenwell & Co. During World War II, Sir Robert was Controller of Communications at the Air Ministry, and Controller of Communications Equipment at the Ministry of Aircraft Production, where he began a close friendship with Mr. Charles Orr-Ewing.

As President of the Television Society, a promotional organization sponsored by equipment manufacturers, Renwick had long advocated the expansion of television services in Britain. As early as 1947 he had urged the Government either to give television more financial support or agree to having sponsored programmes on BBC facilities for a trial period of five years.[27]

Wide-ranging connections in the radio equipment industry,

the financial world, and the Institute of Directors, plus active association with Conservative Party managers combined to make Sir Robert a powerful and effective advocate of commercial television. Some participants in this controversy believed that Renwick's influence in Party circles and with Lord Woolton may have been enhanced by what they assumed to have been his substantial assistance in raising the Conservative Fighting Fund.[28] In speeches and articles Renwick sought to win support for the introduction of commercial television. In one widely reported speech he warned that Britain might be deluged with propaganda by American-owned stations on the Continent. "I know all the technical objections but I also know how far American plans have been advanced."[29] On other occasions he prophesied that ending the BBC's monopoly would result in a tremendous increase in export trade for British goods, that Great Britain could "become the Hollywood of Television provided that the BBC monopoly comes to an end . . ."[30] and he envisioned the production of television films as a vital means of strengthening Commonwealth ties.[31]

The third member of the trio, Mr. C. O. Stanley, was Chairman and Managing Director of Pye, Ltd., a group of nine companies manufacturing radios, television sets and electronic equipment, and a director of some twelve other companies. A former advertising agent and managing director of Arks Publicity, Ltd., Mr. Stanley, after taking over Pye, became one of the most forceful proponents of commercial broadcasting.

As a member of the Radio Industry Council, Mr. Stanley constantly urged that the industry be more outspoken in advocating a rapid expansion of television facilities. The industry had charged the BBC with responsibility for the delay in extending television service, claiming also that "the operation of a television broadcasting monopoly since 1936 has discouraged the radio trade from producing ancillary equipment which is wanted for television studios and transmitting stations."[32] A Labour Government policy of financial stringency and priority for capital investment in vital export industries had in fact been the cause of the delay. When in June, 1949, the Labour Government decided that the BBC might determine its own priorities within the overall total allowed for capital equipment, the BBC decided to plan for 80 per cent national coverage by the end of 1954. This did not satisfy the radio industry, which did not think this was very fast going. "We see no reason why most of the job should not be done by 1952. That is the view we are pressing on the Government."[33] While Chairman of the industry's Television Action Committee, Stanley stressed its determination to do everything possible to bring home to the Government a sense of urgency. One result was that in September, 1949, an all-party delegation of M.P.s met with Sir William Haley and later with the Assistant Postmaster-General to emphasize the need for more television coverage. *

Much of the criticism by those favouring a speedy expansion of television facilities was inaccurately directed against the Television Advisory Committee. In sound broadcasting before the war the BBC had been able to determine its own expansion policy, but in television and VHF sound development after the war the Government appointed a Television Advisory Committee, composed of representatives of the BBC, Government Departments, and the radio industry, to advise the Government on development. This Committee had existed before the war and was reconstituted in October, 1945, and again in October, 1952. With the appointment of the Beveridge Committee its terms of reference were narrowed to prevent overlapping. This action

* The M.P.s deputation to Sir William Haley represented Scotland, North and West England, and Ulster. They had asked that members of the Radio Industry Council be allowed to attend, but Sir William preferred to meet M.P.s only. (*Manchester Guardian*, September 8, 1949.)

was protested by the Radio Industry Council on the grounds "that under its revised terms of reference it will not be possible for the Television Advisory Committee to be effective in developing television in this country."[34] The industry was also dissatisfied with the composition of the Advisory Committee, believing that an insufficient number of independent members meant that the expansion of television was determined by Departmental considerations. This attitude carried over when the Committee was reporting to a Conservative Government.

The powerful restraint on television development was actually the restriction on capital investment imposed by both Labour and Conservative Governments. Absolute orders from the Government permitted the BBC to build only one television transmitter at a time and prevented the Corporation from making commitments for others. The outside interests did not know about these Cabinet rulings and therefore blamed every delay on the Television Advisory Committee and the BBC.

In August, 1952, one of the Conservative backbench "group" wrote to Captain Gammans, Assistant Postmaster-General, that "there are many who feel that [the Advisory Committee] has been a 'stooge' body to give respectability to the BBC plans; the GPO has always provided the Secretariat." In particular, as a deputation to the Postmaster-General stressed on August 21, 1952, they did not believe the Advisory Committee, as then constituted, was the right body to consider the allocation of new television channels. To correct this unfavourable situation they suggested to Captain Gammans that Mr. Norman Collins, Sir Robert Renwick, and Mr. Harold Hobson, a director of General Electric, be appointed to the Advisory Committee.

In October, 1952, Mr. C. O. Stanley and Mr. C. Darnley Smith, chairman of a radio company which was a subsidiary of a Rank film company, were appointed to the Advisory Committee by Postmaster-General Lord De La Warr as representatives of the Radio Industry Council.* Stanley subsequently submitted minority reservations to two reports of the Committee, largely reflecting his opinion that insufficient attention had been given to the question of planning for alternative broadcasting services.†

In July, 1953, with the Government apparently inclined towards an indefinite delay in introducing commercial broadcasting, Mr. Stanley, Mr. Norman Collins, and Sir Robert Renwick actively supported the broadcasting "group" in an intensification of pressure of the Government and individual Conservative Members. By providing both material assistance and renewed enthusiasm they sought to reverse the tide which had begun to turn against them—a reaction largely sparked by widespread disgust with the handling of the Coronation by American commercial television, and intensified by the formation, under most impressive sponsorship, of the National Television Council, a pressure group whose avowed purpose was the defeat of the commercial interests.

* These appointments led to criticism by *Wireless World*, the technical journal: "*Wireless World* has studied the composition of advisory committees in general, and can find nothing approaching a precedent for the state of affairs to which we are now drawing attention. Industrial or commercial interests are not necessarily a barrier to membership; on the contrary, they are sometimes a qualification for it. But the positions of Mr. Darnley Smith and Mr. Stanley, as heads of firms with unique special interests, are quite exceptional, and service on the TAC would subject them to criticism that they should not be asked to bear. Their position is made still more difficult by the fact that although the PMG's statement implies that they represent the Radio Industry Council, we are given to understand that they serve in their personal capacities." (Quoted in H.C. Debs. 525:1487, March 25, 1954.)

† Both reports of the TAC were subjected to scathing attack in Parliament by Mr. C. R. Hobson, Labour Member from Keighley, on the ground that recommended technical changes favoured Pye Radio, Ltd. (H.C. Debs. 525:1488.) See also Mr. Stanley's letter to *The Times*, March 31, 1954.

CHAPTER VII

THE GREAT DEBATE: PR STYLE

ONE OF THE difficulties of writing about any lobby operation, or even some political public relations campaigns directed to achieving specific legislation, is that much of the significant activity is private and submerged. Very often the open manifestation of purpose and activity is the least important aspect of the "engineering of consent"—a diversion to give the illusion of appealing to "public opinion". These characteristics were illustrated in the operations of the two major pressure groups, the National Television Council and the Popular Television Association, quite different alliances which were formed late in the conflict over the introduction of commercial television. There were some similarities in the tactics used by these two organizations, but there were also marked differences in origin, organization, finances, and strategy, as well as, of course, in their declared purpose.

Largely the result of initiative taken by Mr. Christopher Mayhew, Labour M.P. for East Woolwich and free lance producer and writer for the BBC, the National Television Council was formally established on June 18, 1953. A graduate of Haileybury and Christ Church, Oxford, where he had been president of the Union, Mr. Mayhew became professionally active in television following his defeat in the 1950 General Election. Prior to that he had been

Parliamentary Under-Secretary of State for Foreign Affairs. Apparently because the Parliamentary Labour Party's Public Information Group seemed unable to organize effective opposition to the commercial television proposals and, in his judgment, displayed no real sense of urgency, Mr. Mayhew and others who shared his antipathy became convinced that an all-party group outside Parliament was imperative if the commercial plans of the Conservative backbenchers were to be countered.

Though there were many who were disturbed by the revealed intention of the Conservative Government's proposals, there was, until March, 1953, no attempt made by the opposition to organize pressure on the Government to counteract the force being applied by its backbenchers. In part this failure to organize may have stemmed from a widespread feeling that although the Government had accepted commercial television in principle there would be no effort to implement this concession for many years.* It was also apparent that prominent Conservative opponents— Lords Halifax, Brand, Waverley—believed that in such intra-party disputes quiet, off-the-record conversations between "members of the club" could resolve the differences. They probably could not believe that the Government, their Party, was really committed to introduce the vulgarity of commercial television. Only when it became obvious that the Government was once again going to surrender to an implacable minority within its ranks did the opponents of commercial television accept what must have seemed to them the crude method of organizing counter pressure. Certainly it was completely foreign to the experience of these members of "The Establishment" to rely on a propaganda body to resolve internal differences. Top level policy decisions in Great Britain, even less typically than in other countries,

* This despite the fact that on January 21, 1953, the Assistant Postmaster-General had informed the House that the Post Office had received some thirty-four applications for television licences.

were not customarily arrived at by competing appeals to an amorphous "public opinion".

At a meeting of the Parliamentary Labour Party Public Information Group on March 6, 1953, a paper was presented which took for granted the inevitability of commercial television and merely considered proposed safeguards against its abuse. In the discussion which followed, Mr. Mayhew was able to persuade the Group to reject this approach and to intensify their efforts to defeat Conservative plans. No compromise could be acceptable. Members of the Public Information Group were delegated to approach the Archbishop of Canterbury, the Church of Scotland, the Society of Friends and certain other organizations to enlist their formal opposition to commercial television. Mr. Mayhew also announced at this meeting that he was writing a popular pamphlet for wide distribution and that he would make an effort to organize a non-party campaign outside the Parliament against commercial television.

During the spring of 1953, Lord Simon of Wythenshawe, former Chairman of the BBC Board of Governors, began to hold quiet informal luncheons with Mr. Mayhew, Mrs. Mary Stocks who had served on the Beveridge Committee, and others who were concerned about the future of the BBC and the maintenance of public service broadcasting. At one of these lunches in April the decision was reached to attempt an organized campaign against commercial television. Individuals known to be "fanatics" on the subject were to be approached, as well as organizations prepared either to contribute money or moral support to the cause. Originally it was intended that the Association for Education in Citizenship, which had been founded by Lord Simon and therefore thought likely to be sympathetic to his concern, should be used as a highly respectable "front organization". Mr. Gordon Barry, Chairman of the Association, shared the antipathy to commercial broadcasting and had attended several of Lord Simon's lunches. On April 29th it was decided to launch the campaign under the sponsorship of the Association. At the very last moment this plan had to be scrapped when at an Executive Committee meeting on May 29th the Association declined to participate, though for a few weeks they loaned the Association's address to be used for mail purposes.

By the middle of April Mr. Mayhew had completed writing his pamphlet, *Dear Viewer*, and submitted it for criticism to Lord Simon, members of Parliament, officials of the BBC, and other potential supporters. Changes were suggested and made to eliminate any comment that might be considered too politically partisan. A draft copy sent by Mr. Mayhew to Lady Violet Bonham Carter won her warm approval and ultimately led her to agree to work actively for the formation of the non-party group. In a brief conversation in 1952 Mr. Mayhew had learned of her dislike for the commercialization of broadcasting and it was now felt that Lady Violet's status, her political position as a Liberal in touch with the most prominent leaders of the Conservative Party, and her undoubted ability made her an ideal person around whom to build a non-party committee. Some time during this period, Mr. Eric Fletcher, Labour M.P. for East Islington and a Vice-President of Associated British Pictures Corporation, Ltd., informed Mr. Mayhew and Mr. (now Lord) Shackleton, Labour M.P. for Preston South and Chairman of the Parliamentary Public Information Group, that his company would be willing to assist in the anti-commercial television campaign. In particular he offered the part-time services of ABC's public relations officer, Mr. Sydney Lewis, to direct the campaign. After considerable hesitation this offer was accepted because of sheer financial necessity, with the understanding that the new organization would be under no obligation of any kind to promote the policy of the cinema industry.

As a result of extended conversations between Lord Simon and Messrs. Mayhew, Shackleton, Lewis and Barry, it was decided to invite a number of people to form the National Television Council. The Mayhew pamphlet, which was to become the most widely distributed statement of the organization's case, had been submitted to the *News Chronicle* for their consideration, but after some deliberation the paper decided against publishing it. Since the group did not want the pamphlet published by a left-wing firm, Mr. Mayhew finally accepted the offer of Messrs. Lincolns Prager. Negotiations were no doubt facilitated by the willingness of Sir Philip Warter, Chairman of ABC Ltd., to buy 50,000 copies immediately. On May 19th Mr. Mayhew and Mr. (now Sir) Gerald Barry met with Lady Violet Bonham Carter and proposed that the National Television Council be formed by inviting some fifty distinguished people to a private meeting for that purpose at her home. Lady Violet accepted the draft of a letter of invitation and agreed that Lords Brand, Halifax, and Waverley, Mr. Tom O'Brien, Labour M.P. and Chairman of the TUC, and the Archbishop of York be asked to join her in signing it. She also agreed to write Lord Waverley, who had shown some reluctance to participate. Lords Halifax and Brand readily agreed to the use of their names, which helped persuade Lord Waverley to go along. Though the Archbishop of York declined the use of his name, he expressed his support and his willingness to speak in support of the Council.

Just at this time, when it looked as though the Council would be launched under these most impressive auspices, the Assistant Postmaster-General made a statement in the House of Commons that thoroughly alarmed opponents of commercial television.[1] He promised the House that there would be a comprehensive statement of the Government's policy when Parliament reconvened in October. Immediately there was widespread speculation on the early granting of licences to commercial broadcasting firms. Certainly to the opponents it appeared obvious that the Government was taking crucial decisions and that the planned formation of the National Television Council might well come too late. The sponsors therefore decided that they had no choice but to announce their intention of forming the Council immediately by means of a letter to *The Times*. A letter was drafted and sent to the sponsors for approval. Sir William Haley, editor of *The Times*, suggested that its publication be delayed until after the Coronation on June 2nd, so it finally appeared on June 4th over the signatures of Lady Violet Bonham Carter, Lord Brand, Lord Halifax, Mr. Tom O'Brien, and Lord Waverley. The letter read as follows:

Sir,

Recent statements in the House of Commons make it clear that the question of commercial television is becoming an urgent one. The report of the Television Advisory Committee has been received and is being considered by the Government. Various newspapers have already applied for a licence for commercial television; and a statement of the Government's intentions is to be made soon after Parliament reassembles on June 9th.

It has also been announced recently that no less than 2,142,452 viewers now hold licences for television sets, and that this figure is expected to increase at the rate of 600,000 a year. Before very long, therefore, most of the population of Great Britain, including millions of children, are likely to have become regular viewers. We believe that the development of this new medium of information and entertainment calls for the exercise of the highest sense of social responsibility in all those engaged in it, and that commercialization—now imminently threatened—is fraught with dangers to those spiritual and intellectual values which the BBC has nobly striven to maintain.

We express our sincere hope that the Government will yield no further to the intense pressure to which they have been subjected by a comparatively small number of interested parties; and that they will decide, even at this last moment, to remain true to the principles which have given us the finest broadcasting system in the world.

In the belief that these issues should be more widely understood, we are hoping shortly to form a National Television Council. The aims of the council will be to resist the introduction of commercial television into this country, and to encourage the healthy development of public-service television in the national interest. We would be glad to hear from any of your readers who feel they could help us. They should reply to the Campaign Secretary, 14, Kendall Place, London, W.1.

For its impact the letter could not have been better timed. It was generally agreed that the BBC's telecast of the coronation was superb, the best of its very skilful outside broadcasts, and the most widely seen both in Britain and throughout the world. The full year of planning and preparation had paid off. Never had the Corporation's prestige been higher. More than twenty million adults saw the programme as for the first time a British television audience was larger than for radio. At the same time, American commercial broadcasting was bitterly criticized by the British Press because some stations interjected advertising comment with sequences of the coronation ceremony and one station managed to introduce J. Fred Muggs, a chimpanzee, into the act.* The

* In particular, criticisms were levelled at the interruption of the communion ceremony to advertise "Pepperell's Bed Sheets," cars (General Motors showed a collection of its badges as "America's Crown Jewels," and another car was described as "Queen of the Road"), soap, salad oil, jewellery and deodorant. One commentator suggested that "Basil Radford could have played the part of the Archbishop of Canterbury." (See Alistair Buchan in *The Observer*, June 7, 1953; Cassandra in the *Daily Mirror*, June 9, 1953; *Daily Express*, June 9, 1953; *The Times*, June 8, 1953; *Daily Express*, June 7, 1953.) Critical reaction was intensified when Mr. Hugh Carleton Greene, then Assistant Controller of the BBC

result was to intensify interest in a letter calling for the formation of a group to oppose the introduction of commercial broadcasting in Britain. Some two hundred and fifty letters of support for the new organization were received from prominent people, with an additional two hundred letters when a slightly modified version of the appeal was re-published in *The Observer*. At the same time, fifty letters were dispatched, with a covering letter from Lady Violet, with invitations to the foundation meeting of the Council to be held on June 18, 1953, at her home.

Some twenty persons attended the meeting, some in an individual capacity, others as officials and spokesmen for organizations. The meeting approved the following resolution:

"That for the purpose of resisting commercial television and encouraging the healthy development of public-service television in the national interest, a National Television Council is hereby formed."

An Organizing Committee with executive power to act for the Council and to co-opt additional members was appointed and an extensive list of vice-presidents approved. Viscount Waverley had consented to serve as honorary president and Lady Violet Bonham Carter subsequently agreed to serve as active Chairman of the Organizing Committee. The most active members of this Committee, which met every two weeks in an interview room at the House of Commons, included Mr. Christopher Mayhew, Mr. Edward Shackleton, Miss Elise Sprott, an executive of the National Council of

---

Overseas Service, stated that "We had a definite gentleman's agreement with the U.S. television networks that the ceremony in the Abbey should be free of commercial plugs of any kind, and that during the rest of the procession they should use their discretion." (*Daily Mail*, June 8, 1953.)

Women of Great Britain, Lady Violet Bonham Carter, Mr. Gordon Barry, Chairman of the Association for Education in Citizenship, Mr. Frederick Carter, of Prince Littler Productions, Ltd., the Reverend Edward Rodgers, Methodist Church Department of Christian Citizenship, and Mrs. Mary Stocks. There were two members representing the Liberal Party, Mr. Philip Fothergill and Mr. D. W. Wade, M.P. In February, 1954, Lord Hailsham, later Chairman of the Conservative Party, joined the Organizing Committee. He had previously been active as a vice-president, working closely with the executive and speaking on behalf of the organization. Mr. Sydney K. Lewis, whose services had been loaned to the Council by Associated British Pictures Corporation, served as executive secretary. *

Throughout the controversy and before the formation of the National Television Council, proponents of commercial television had criticized the advocates of public service broadcasting for having a vested interest motivation—apparently with the idea that a strong offence was the best defence. It is true that many of the leading figures had served as Governors or members of the BBC Advisory Committees, and Mr. Mayhew was a highly successful broadcaster. However, to an outsider it appears that the vast majority of affiliated individuals and organizations were certainly disinterested in any economic sense. Even political advantage was doubtful for a Labour M.P. or a trade union leader, since there was some evidence to suggest that commercial radio and the prospect of commercial television had more appeal among potential Labour voters. There were exceptions—the Associated British Picture Corporation, the West End Theatre Managers, Ltd., the Cinematograph Exhibitors Association, the National Association of Cinematograph & Allied Technicians. These groups certainly anticipated that cinema and theatre would suffer from the competition of commercial

* No secret was ever made of this fact, as see note in *Today's Cinema*, June 22, 1953.

television. To this extent one may suspect the sincerity of
their devotion to public service broadcasting. They did not,
however, determine policy or influence the tactics of the
Council.

Those who directed activities, conducted public meetings,
and bore the brunt of routine work did so without expectation
of gain and, in fact, at considerable personal sacrifice.
Speakers for the National Television Council were not paid
and examination of the financial records does not reveal any
remuneration for those who wrote pamphlets. Actually Mr.
Mayhew contributed the royalties from the sale of his
pamphlet to the Council.

An effective "grass roots" campaign aimed at arousing
masses of people in constituencies throughout the country
is an extremely costly operation requiring highly skilled,
possibly cynical talent and extensive organization. This
approach seems never to have been considered by the
Council. It was never intended that the Council should
become a large membership organization. Its organizers
counted on the "weight of authority" to influence the
Cabinet, individual Conservative M.P.s, and insure adequate
Press coverage for its case. To a considerable extent the
Council was a "letterhead" organization, though this is not
to imply that its sponsors were not in complete agreement
and fully informed of its activity. From the beginning the
Council received support from individuals and organizations
representative of religious, cultural, educational, professional, business and trade union concern. Ultimately, 350
individuals and scores of organizations acquired membership
either through money donations or by contributing some
service to the cause. In a sense the alliance already existed
before the Council was formed, for many organizations had
registered their opposition to commercial television with
the Beveridge Committee and scores of individuals had
condemned the Government's proposals in letters to the
Press. The immediate concern of the Council was to organize

and channel this already existing support. It may be that one of the explanations of the relative failure of the Council's effort was that it appealed to, and spoke for, the already converted and achieved little impact on the uncommitted.

Finances of the Council were limited, in part, at least, by a self-denying decision to accept donations from any individual or organization, "but not to such an extent that any one particular person, body of persons, or Association was predominant" or had any influence on policy matters. There were few large donations, with the largest £250, and at least one of these came from a body not in any way connected with the Council. More important than financial considerations in determining the kind of campaign conducted was the composition of the Council. The diverse political support, the philosophy, convictions and social background of those who formulated policy inevitably determined the kind of tactics utilized. Judged by professional public relations standards, the campaign was restrained, even amateurish, not in quality but in conception. All publications, letters to newspapers, Press releases and meetings were identified as originating with the National Television Council.* The Organizing Committee met regularly to approve publications, decide upon activity, and issue Press statements commenting on Government plans. All important questions of policy and some tactical considerations were referred to the President, Lord Waverley, and some of the vice-presidents. Thus, when an emergency meeting of the Committee decided to issue a Press release commenting on a Government television policy statement, it was phoned to Lord Waverley for his approval before it was given to the Press Association.

* Some members of the Conservative backbench "Group" charged that the National Television Council had "representatives in the U.S.A. [who] had been asked to comb the United States television broadcasts for lapses of taste which could be used in supporting the campaign to maintain the monopoly." (Memorandum, dated November 19, 1953.)

F

In September, 1953, the question of the desirability of sending a delegation to the Prime Minister was referred to Lords Waverley, Halifax and Brand for decision and, as it turned out, rejection, on the grounds that it should wait on the publication of the promised White Paper.

A voluntary speakers' panel was formed which included most of the members of the Organizing Committee, as well as some Council supporters from universities and other educational bodies. Altogether some forty-five meetings were addressed at university debating societies, political clubs, youth centres, citizens' associations, chambers of trade, Workers' Educational Association groups, and Rotary Clubs. Several debates with Popular Television representatives were staged: Lord Hailsham sharing a platform at Caxton Hall, London, with Mr. Ted Kavanagh; Mr. Mayhew and Mr. Norman Collins at the Oxford Union; and Lady Violet Bonham Carter and Mr. Malcolm Muggeridge holding forth before the '51 Society on the BBC.

The Council had easy access to the national Press, especially to *The Times*, which had always supported the BBC's monopoly, *The Observer*, and the *Manchester Guardian*, partly because of the prestige of its supporters and because the newspapers, with the principal exception of the *Daily Mirror* group, were hostile to commercial television. The Press had historically opposed any use of radio as an advertising medium and before the Beveridge Committee the Newspaper Proprietors' Association, Ltd., restated this opposition. Newspapers had originally refused to publish BBC programme schedules, which led to publication of *Radio Times*, and most papers ignored Continental station announcements. Beyond this commercial rivalry, papers like *The Times* and *The Observer* were staunch supporters of the BBC. Sir William Haley had resigned as Director-General of the BBC to become editor of *The Times* and Mr. William Clark, an editorial writer and Parliamentary correspondent for *The Observer* had been intimately involved in the formation of the National Television Council. The Council received less support from many of the provincial papers and weeklies which were more susceptible to the deluge of free material which poured out of the Popular Television Association, the rival group. The Organizing Committee and the Executive Secretary carefully watched the national Press and made certain that a rejoinder was given on any vital points raised by the opposition. Members of the Council performed as volunteer Press watchers of the local and regional papers to see that the Council's position was represented.

Three major pamphlets were distributed, Mr. Mayhew's *Dear Viewer* having the largest circulation at 60,000 and representing the most complete statement of the Council's policy. Following the second Conservative White Paper in November, 1953, the Council published *Britain Unites Against Commercial Television*, and in December, just before the debate in the House of Commons, they released *Public Opinion Reflected By the Press*. This literature was sent to every Member of the House of Lords and House of Commons, to members of the National Television Council, to newspapers throughout the country and to a considerable number of organizations. A number of organizations requested pamphlets for distribution to their own members. Thus the Methodist Church Department of Christian Citizenship sent copies to every Methodist Minister in the country.

Considerable attention was devoted to persuading organizations not directly affiliated with the Council to pass resolutions condemning commercial television and send them to the Prime Minister and the Postmaster-General. Many of these bodies, especially the religious and educational organizations, would have passed such resolutions in any case as standard operating procedure, but certainly a flood of them poured in on the Government. Sympathetic groups were also urged to influence their members to write to their M.P.s, especially where they were represented by Conservatives.

Not surprisingly, given the status of many of its vice-presidents and their connections in the business and social world, a good share of the Council's work took the form of personal appeals for support to other influential individuals. Approaches were made to Chambers of Commerce and Trade and to individual manufacturers and advertisers known to be reluctant to become involved in additional advertising expenditure. On the political level, attempts were made to persuade some Conservative Members to oppose the Government, or at the least to urge that a free vote on the issue be permitted. Before the debate in the House of Lords, November 25-26, 1953, Mr. Sydney Lewis sent out a letter on behalf of Lord Halifax requesting all Peers to attend the debate and support Lord Halifax's motion condemning the Government's White Paper. Members of the Organizing Committee were present at this debate, as they were for the Commons debate, and they and the office staff were available for any information or assistance required by the participants.

In July, 1953, a second pressure group was formed to organize support for the introduction of commercial television. The origins of this body, the Popular Television Association, are not agreed upon even by those who participated in its formation and directed its activities. Thus Mr. Ronald Simms, the Association's full-time secretary and later successor to Mr. Mark Chapman-Walker as publicity director for the Conservative Party, told the Press on July 22, 1953, that the idea for such an organization had originated with the Earl of Derby who had agreed to serve as its President. [2] Mr. Simms, a prospective Conservative candidate, had been seconded from the advertising agency, W. H. Gollings & Associates, to direct the Association's work. He felt able to assure newspaper reporters at the first Press conference that "we have no financial connection with commercial TV." [3] Subsequently, Mr. Simms recalled that "a number of public-spirited men, led by the Earl of Derby, decided that the dictatorial spirit associated with the BBC monopoly should be fought, and so the Popular Television Association was formed."[4] And in a letter to the *Lancashire Evening Post* Mr. Simms wrote: "I can categorically assure . . . that this Association is not 'a cloak to cover the activities of an advertising medium'."[5] Lord Foley, pianist and composer active on behalf of commercial television since the Lords' debate in 1946 and a vice-president of the Popular Television Association, assured a Liverpool audience "that the Association's members had no direct interest in competitive television and had formed the Association with no political or financial interest."[6] Presumably it was the recollection of this non-partisan origin of the Popular Television Association which inspired Lord Derby's rebuke to Mr. Tom O'Brien, Labour M.P. for Northwest Nottingham, secretary of the National Association of Theatrical Kine Employees, and a vice-president of the National Television Council, for his opposition to commercial television. "Mr. O'Brien's attack," said Lord Derby, "is scarcely impartial."[7]

A somewhat different version of Popular Television's origins was recalled in 1959 by Lord Woolton, who was in 1953 the Chairman of the Conservative Party. "We created the Popular Television Association—you know, ex-Central Office—" he told the writer, "and put Lord Derby at the head of it."[8] This was done, according to a Conservative Central Office spokesman, because it was thought desirable to have a non-party organization to counteract the efforts of the National Television Council. "This," he suggested, "is a common practice of the Conservative Party. It was done before and has been done since the television controversy."[9] Other participants recall additional organizational aspects. Following the call to form the National Television Council by so distinguished a list of sponsors, the proponents of commercial television were disheartened and some were pretty well convinced that their cause was hopeless. Several individuals were prepared to drop out of the controversy rather than appear publicly as opponents of Lord Halifax, the Archbishops, and University Vice-Chancellors. It was also generally believed that the Cabinet had been quite shaken by the formidable opposition to its plans and the wide-spread public reaction against the "vulgar" handling of the coronation broadcast by some American stations. In fact, many of those supporting the continuation of the BBC and public service broadcasting unchanged were convinced in July, 1953, that their fight had been won and that the Government would have to retreat.

This evaluation seemed to be supported by the simultaneous announcement of the Government's intentions in the House of Lords and House of Commons on Wednesday, July 2, 1953. * Though standing by its year-old commitment to introduce "some element of competition" in broadcasting, there was evident a cautiousness that outraged Conservative back-benchers and heartened the supporters of public service broadcasting.† Lord De La Warr, Postmaster-General, stated—and a similar statement was made in the Commons by Mr. H. F. C. Crookshank, Leader of the House—that the BBC was authorized to proceed at once with an expansion that would enable it to reach another six to seven million viewers, as well as starting Very High Frequency sound broadcasting to improve reception in areas not adequately served. To provide more opportunity for public discussion the Government intended to publish a White Paper in the autumn defining the terms upon which "competitive

* An editorial reaction to this announcement in the *Daily Express* somewhat prematurely announced that "Commercial TV died yesterday." (July 3, 1953.)

† Guy Eden, writing in *Truth*, July 10, 1953, observed: "I have seldom seen Tory backbenchers so openly angry with their own Government—they muttered and wriggled in rage and yelled 'might!' with ferocious emphasis when Mr. Crookshank used that word in connexion with the prospects of Commercial TV licences being granted."

television *might* be permitted to operate." In any case, the BBC would remain intact and "its scope will be extended. Its national and international standing will be unaffected, and its revenue and present basis of work will remain secure." The broad principles to govern the system that "might be set up" further alarmed the proponents of commercial broadcasting. For Lord De La Warr said that the number of stations under any one ownership or control would be limited; a controlling body would be set up to advise the Postmaster-General on licences and programme standards, with power "to call for a script in advance of presentation," and to make recommendations to the Postmaster-General for the suspension or withdrawal of any particular licence. The licence or the controlling body might also specify the maximum number of broadcasting hours, restrictions on the advertising of certain products, and the percentage of time and the place allotted to advertising in any programme.

The immediate result of the Government's announcement was a meeting of interested Conservative backbenchers on July 3rd to discuss its implications and the strategy to be followed. According to some of those present, majority opinion wanted commercial television introduced as rapidly as possible. On July 9th, this view was conveyed to the 1922 Committee, and the Chancellor of the Exchequer promised the Members that the Government would speed plans for the introduction of commercial television.* At this time, too, the Broadcasting Group was reconstituted as a Radio and Television Committee with Mr. Walter Elliott as chairman, Sir Robert Grimston as vice-chairman, and Lord John Hope as honorary secretary. This was a definite gain because of

* Some Conservative M.P.s did support the Government policy of delay. Mr. Anthony Hurd, M.P. for Newbury, speaking in his constituency on Saturday, July 11th, said that even though some Conservative backbenchers were impatient to force the pace, the Cabinet was right to wait for more public opinion to form. (*The Observer*, July 12, and *The Times*, July 13, 1953.)

the new chairman's reputation for moderation and it gave the committee status as a Permanent Party Committee.*

The second result of the Government's cautious approach was a decision to intensify pressure on the Cabinet. Those who had secured the original commitment had expected that commercial television would be licensed within a few months of the publication of the May, 1952, White Paper. They now felt that their failure to continue pressure on the Government had permitted what one of them called, "the prudes, prigs, and priests" to develop a successful counter-attack.† It was therefore decided to widen the front against a reluctant Government and to make an effort to neutralize the increasing hostility of influential persons and organizations towards any proposal to introduce commercial broadcasting. They were supported in this decision by Mr. C. O. Stanley, Sir Robert Renwick, and Mr. Norman Collins. Once this course of action was decided upon, Lord Woolton requested the Earl of Bessborough to ask the Earl of Derby to head the new organization.[10]

On July 16, 1953, Lord Bessborough, at his invitation, met at the Turf Club with Lord Derby, Mr. Norman Collins, and Mr. Mark Chapman-Walker. At this meeting Lord Derby, who was later to become President of Television Wales and West, agreed to serve as President of the Popular Television Association. A week later the organization was formed at a meeting held at St. Stephens Club and attended by the Conservative Broadcasting Group, Sir Robert Renwick, and Mr. C. O. Stanley. According to the recollections of individuals present, some £20,000 was

---

* The *Manchester Guardian*, July 9, 1953, commented: "There has already been great activity among Tory backbenchers anxious to promote commercial television but their work has been unofficial."

† *Manchester Guardian*, July 3, 1953. It is interesting that this period of let-up of pressure was coincident with Lord Woolton's incapacitation due to a perforated appendix. He was stricken in October, 1952, at the Party Conference in Scarborough and did not resume his duties until April, 1953. (*Memoirs*, p. 402, 414.)

raised at this gathering to implement the campaign for commercial television. The first Press conference of the new Association was held on July 22nd, and a letter to *The Times*, signed by L. J. Collins, Joan Davidson, Derby, Malcolm Muggeridge, and Arnold Plant, declared their concern with "the dangers of a monopoly in the field of television" and their conviction "that competitive programmes should be made available to the public as soon as possible."[11] It was the intention of the Popular Television Association to bring pressure to bear on the Cabinet and undecided Conservative Members by stimulating, or simulating, a public demand for commercial television. * To this end, unlike the National Television Council, the directors sought to create a mass organization, ultimately claiming a membership of 10,000 to 12,000.† The announced non-party and public service nature of the organization enabled the initiators to acquire an array of vice-presidents, including the usual assortment of titles, two or three churchmen, university professors, a cricketer and a few writers.

Never was the Association able to gain the kind of prestige support that had rallied to the defence of the BBC and worked with the National Television Council. Though few knew the origins of the Association, there had been since 1950 sufficient Press discussion of the vested interest origins of the commercial campaign to make even critics of the BBC wary of affiliation. Some of the more prominent supporters with no economic stake in the outcome had no illusions about

---

* The *Daily Sketch*, on July 23, 1953, commented on the formation of the Popular Television Association: It "will stump the country presenting the case for competitive television—'not sponsored', please. . . . With the idea of getting a favourable reaction when the Government's promised White Paper is debated in the autumn, P.T.A. is going to lobby M.P.s."

† Because of the Association's policy of secrecy it was not possible to verify these figures. As reported in the London *Evening Standard* on March 6, 1954, Mr. Ronald Simms referred to the Association's "5,000 members".

F*

the financial backing for the Association, but were so hostile
to the BBC that they would have used any means to break its
control of British broadcasting. Thus, Professor A. J. P.
Taylor had written to the *New Statesman* to assert that "it
is untrue that the demand for free television comes solely
from 'a small pressure group'."[12] The fact was, he thought,
that everyone with any BBC experience favoured an alternative. He knew that the money for Popular Television came
from "C. O. Stanley and other radio equipment manufacturers," but saw no reason not to use it in "a good cause".
He did not know that the Association had been created by the
Conservative Central Office.[13]

The declared object of the Popular Television Association
was:

> "To awaken the national conscience to the dangers,
> social, political and artistic, of monopoly in the rapidly
> expanding field of television, to provide the public at the
> earliest possible moment with alternative programmes
> which are in keeping with the best standards of British taste
> and to open up steadily widening opportunities of employ-
> ment for artists, writers, producers, and technicians in all
> fields of the entertainment and electronics industries."

In furtherance of these unexceptionable aims the Popular
Television Association launched an intensive campaign to
flood all the available media. They relied upon tactics which
had been operationally tested by the Economic League, the
Aims of Industry, and the Woolton propaganda brains trust.

Although refusing to disclose details of their financial
support or expenditures on the campaign, beyond saying that
the bulk of the contributions "came from radio/television
manufacturers," the nature and extent of the campaign
conducted by Popular Television illustrates that it was not
restricted by financial stringency. Pamphlets were produced
and distributed in thousands to present the Association's
case for commercial television, which was delicately

described as "Competitive Television". They were skilfully written to focus on the emotional antipathy to monopoly. The Association had no quarrel with the BBC, but only feared the potential danger of monopoly in "a medium of unexampled impact and therefore of unexampled power." Any suspicion of commercial motive was dispelled by the obvious dedication of the Association to intellectual and cultural freedom. "It is the aim of the Popular Television Association to help in the task of setting television free. For all who value freedom of the mind, there is no more important task today."* They appealed to a natural desire of viewers for an additional programme, more viewing time, "much higher quality and a much greater variety of programmes" than could be provided by a monopoly, and all this "at no cost to the public."

As is usual in professionally conducted public relations campaigns, the vast bulk of the propaganda was disseminated as "news", not identified as Association handouts. To a mailing list of 1,400 newspapers, the Association sent a stream of feature articles written under newsworthy names. A panel of writers was gathered to produce articles, or to allow their names to be used on stories designed to promote commercial television. The panel included, among others, Mr. David Hardman, Labour M.P. for Darlington 1945-50 and Parliamentary Secretary to the Ministry of Education; Mr. Alec Bedser, Surrey and England fast bowler; Mr. Maurice Winnick, former band leader and owner of the British broadcasting rights to "What's My Line?" and later unsuccessful contender for a commercial television licence; Mr. Gillie Potter, a former BBC radio comedian; Mr. Ted Kavanagh, famous as the scriptwriter for the

* One of their speakers, Major C. H. Tait, found the BBC the worst kind of monopoly because "it set out unashamedly to make people think, and from that it was only a short step to telling them what to think." (*Richmond & Twickenham Times*, November 27, 1953.)

tremendously popular "ITMA" series on the BBC; and Professor A. J. P. Taylor, sprightly Oxford historian and bitter critic of the BBC who had become a television personality as a result of his appearance on the panel in "In the News". Many provincial papers printed these stories without indicating their source. A few papers refused to co-operate. Thus, the *Aldershot News*[14] commented: "During the last six months there has appeared in the post of this newspaper every week pages and pages of foolscap publicity material written under names famous in the entertainment world, and which were intended to be published to boost Popular Television. With them have been sketches and features and offers and types of many kinds of publicity from the Popular Television Association. None of this material has been used. . . ."[15] Other papers were less inhibited about accepting the handouts. Thus an article bearing the name of Mr. David Hardman supporting commercial television and "correcting" erroneous views of American television appeared in the *Voice of Industry*, November, 1953, the *Irish Times Pictorial*, September 23-30, 1953, the *Shields Gazette*, September 25, 1953, and the *Dumfries & Galloway Standard*, September 23, 1953. An unsigned personal promotional piece on the Earl of Derby appeared in at least a dozen newspapers with no indication of its source.

Characteristically, every criticism of the BBC, whatever its origin, was written up by the Association and sent out to the newspapers.* For example, there was a claim that the BBC was unable to obtain the services of the most popular performers because they didn't pay enough and because poor BBC producing damaged the artists' reputations. "To

---

* The form letter sent out to those who joined the Association concluded: "If BBC programmes fail to come up to standard, bring the subject up with your friends. Above all, keep hammering home the advantages of good alternative competitive programmes. Eventually, no doubt, we shall have our way and, with it, better viewing."

put the situation at its mildest the outlook for viewers is not so good." This identical story appeared in at least a score of papers. There were repeated accounts of a forthcoming increase in the BBC licence fee; a claim by comedian Gillie Potter that the BBC was "flogging foul films and boosting bawdy books" was widely distributed, as was an editorial, "Soothing", which suggested that although "viewers have been known to say that some of the BBC programmes nearly drive them mad," dull BBC television had been found to be soothing for mental patients. When Mr. Norman Collins attacked the "Brahmin caste" of BBC broadcasters and claimed that the Corporation had turned down £1 million a year for the use of facilities not then being used, it was headlined in papers across the country. A Third Programme "error" of broadcasting excerpts from George Barker's poem, "Passages from True Confessions", was condemned by Lord Balfour of Inchrye, a sponsor of Popular Television, in the House of Lords as "a piece of pornography which should never have been printed let alone read." Subsequently, Sir Alexander Cadogan, Chairman of the BBC Board of Governors, wrote a letter of apology to Lord Balfour agreeing that the poem should not have been broadcast. This story was sent out by the Association to papers all over the country. As a result of the feature and news stories, as well as the editorials sent out for the editors' use, the Association was able to "claim to have secured a total of just over a thousand column inches of editorial space in a recent week."[16]

An extensive letter-to-the-editor campaign was inspired, with Association literature urging its supporters to write letters "to the Press, calling for the immediate introduction of Comp8etititive Television." In case any of its sympathizers found difficulty in composing an appropriate letter, the Association volunteered assistance. "If any members would like draft letters to send to their local papers, we will gladly supply them," a tactic which was characterized in *Worlds Press News*[17] as "a whole new nitwit industry." However described, the technique did produce interesting results. For example, very similar letters with some identical paragraphs appeared in the *Lewisham Boro' News*, September 15, 1953, signed by "H. D. Taylor, Whitefoot Ward Conservatives, 35 Brangbourne Road, Catford," in the *Walthamstow Guardian*, September 18, 1953, signed "B. L. Morgan, Chairman, Chingford Conservative Association," and in the *Isle of Man Daily Times*, October 20, 1953, signed by Ronald Simms. An identical letter appeared in at least twenty-two newspapers signed variously, "M. Awan," "M. A. Warr," "M. Adam," "M. Swan," "M. Ardan," but always listing the same address. Another letter purporting to be from a Labour Party member wanted to know why "I should be compelled to oppose a piece of [Conservative] legislation which I consider to be highly desirable. In my view this country not only wants commercial television it needs it." The letter, which appeared in at least nineteen provincial newspapers, was signed "Leonard London", and the address given was that of a secretarial bureau in Vauxhall Bridge Road, London. Such anonymity was not always approved by the Popular Television Association, for Mr. Simms condemned one individual critical of commercial television for signing his letter to the *Mosley Advertiser*, "Viewer". If letters-to-the-editor are interpreted to indicate keen public interest, this letter manufacturing tactic was a success, as suggested by Mr. Simms when he wrote to the editor of the *Advertisers' Weekly*.[18] Refuting the contention of a correspondent that there had been no popular demand for commercial television, Mr. Simms said, "I disagree wholeheartedly. I receive a large number of provincial papers and have noticed in the past few weeks a tremendous increase in the number of letters in these papers putting the case of people who genuinely desire to have alternative services."

Unlike the National Television Council, there was little formal or public organizational support for the Popular Television Association. Though the Association had plenty

of allies, most of them were undeclared. Thus, some advertising agencies and individual agency officials contributed
funds to the Association but they did not openly affiliate. In
fact, Mr. John Rodgers, Conservative M.P. and a director of
J. Walter Thompson, recalls that he had nothing to do with
the Popular Television Association because "that was set
up by vested interests."[19] There was, however, a close
working relationship with the Aims of Industry, a public
relations firm which had established its reputation in the
course of conducting the Tate & Lyle anti-nationalization
campaign in 1950. Co-operation in the effort to obtain
commercial television was facilitated by an established understanding with the Conservative Central Office and by personnel borrowed from Aims of Industry. Mr. Kenneth Mason
and Mr. Gordon McIvor were seconded from Aims, which
was paid for their services by Popular Television. Mr. Mc-
Ivor succeeded Ronald Simms as Secretary of the Association
when the latter moved on to become publicity officer for the
Conservative Party. Aims of Industry co-operated in the
distribution of propaganda material, handled feature and
news stories, provided films, and made available the services
of their panel of "free lance lecturers" who normally spoke
for clients of Aims of Industry. Now billed as experts on
television and paid an average of four guineas a meeting,
these speakers appeared before Chambers of Commerce,
Young Conservative clubs, and Rotary Clubs throughout the
country.[20] In addition, the commercial television campaign
used ten indoor film units which Mr. McIvor estimated to
have reached an audience of at least 225,000, and for six
months they had two outdoor film vans which toured cities
and holiday resorts from Scotland to the south coast and may
have reached another 200,000 people. A twelve-minute film
entitled "Television Choice" featured interviews with the
Earl of Derby, Canon C. B. Mortlock, Alec Bedser, Joan
Griffiths and others. These vans also distributed literature
and membership forms which gave the Association's view a

wide distribution. Some eight formal public meetings were held in London, Birmingham, Cardiff, Liverpool, Glasgow, Edinburgh, Manchester, and York.

Throughout the campaign, speakers for Popular Television made promises to various cultural, sectional, and occupational interests. For the religious, Lord Derby revealed in an interview with Mr. Ernest Moore of the *Lancashire Evening Post* that television "in America has helped a religious revival. It can also help in this way in our own country." Mr. Ted Kavanagh implied that with commercial television more time would be made available for Catholic broadcasts.* To a Glasgow audience, Mr. Ronald Simms announced that since "you are, as a whole, more intelligent than the rest of the country," Scotland "should have priority when commercial TV licences are granted. We believe that until now insufficient attention has been paid to this country's claim for a good and localized service."[21] And in a Press conference at Cardiff, Simms announced that within a short time after the licensing of the first commercial station Wales would have its own national television service.[22] To those who feared that commercial television would mean low standards, Association spokesmen suggested that "probably reputable bodies like universities would be given licences to operate stations,"[23] and Lord Foley told a Manchester audience that "it is rather nice to think that we might even have the Hallé [Orchestra] running its own station."[24]

During the debate on the BBC, opponents of change had warned that commercial broadcasting inevitably would mean

---

* *Scottish Catholic Herald*, October 30, 1953. In a letter to the *Catholic Herald*, July 10, 1953, Colm Brogan, a sponsor of the Popular Television Association, had written: ". . . It is entirely possible that we could have our Catholic stations in time, not merely occasional Catholic programmes. Is it wise of Catholics to support a State monopoly which will limit our employment of this instrument of infinite potentialities to what a non-Catholic and largely secular authority may be willing to allow us?"

interruption of programmes by advertising. Since many people disliked this prospect, Association spokesmen sought to counteract this criticism. In demonstrations at radio and television exhibitions they presented innocuous versions of what advertising support would entail: "The following concert is being presented by. . . ." and "You have just heard a concert sponsored by. . . ." Beyond this, the Association, both in its leaflets and through speakers asserted: "There will be advertising announcements at the beginning or the end of a programme, but there will never be any interruptions."[25] Mr. Norman Collins, the most persuasive and moderate spokesman for commercial television, guaranteed his audiences that "there will be no overlong or interruptive advertising."[26]

In speeches and widely distributed articles, Lord Derby, Sir Robert Renwick, and other representatives of the Association heralded a tremendous expansion of British industry that would accompany the introduction of commercial television. As headlined in the *Glasgow Evening Times*[27] "Commercial TV Would Mean More Work For Thousands." There would be, according to this prognosis, an unprecedented export market for British cameras, studio equipment, control rooms, transmitters and other technical equipment. At home, in addition to all the workers needed by the radio industry itself, the building industry would gain from the demand for regional studios and transmitting stations. Furthermore, Lord Derby informed a London Press conference, unlike the BBC, commercial television would not borrow ideas for programmes from the United States. "We have a vast source of talent in this country and the entertainment will be substantially British, giving employment to thousands of actors, actresses and technicians."[28] To whet interest and mobilize this talent, the Association's secretary Mr. Simms sent letters or notices to all the specialized journals catering to the professional interests of artists, actors, composers, scriptwriters, magicians, and designers.

Typical was the notice appearing in *Melody Maker*[29] headlined, "Songwriters Ready for the Rush": "In anticipation of
sponsored television, the Popular TV Association is preparing a list of composers and lyric writers which will be
made available to bona fide advertisers."[30] The *Dublin
Sunday Express*[31] carried Mr. Simms' discovery that "television organizations are looking for more Irish people . . .
Irish people who can write, who are artists, musicians,
producers, entertainers, designers or actors." As a service
to this talent the Popular Television Association was, said
Simms, "preparing lists of such people willing to work for
competitive television." In 1959, when asked what use has
been made of these various lists of talented individuals, Mr.
Gordon McIvor, successor to Ronald Simms, said they
"might" have been passed on to the programme companies,
"but really they were just a gimmick to win support."[32]

Despite the lists of prominent speakers offered by both
groups, and despite the varying tactics used to attract
attention, the public was generally apathetic and did not
attend the public meetings sponsored by either pressure
group. In one instance at Chingford, for example, six hundred
invitations were sent out by the sponsoring organization and
nine persons attended the meeting. At Manchester, a meeting
scheduled by the YMCA was cancelled following the failure
of a Popular Television Association meeting to attract an
audience. Professor A. J. P. Taylor, who participated in a
well-publicized meeting in the Birmingham Town Hall
featuring six speakers, recalled that only about thirty people
turned up.[33] This lack of enthusiasm with which the efforts
of both groups were greeted tends to substantiate the conclusion that both groups failed in the attempt to galvanize
public opinion on the issue. It is true that the National
Television Council did not envision itself as a mass organization and did not direct its appeals to the masses. It is also true
that, as mentioned before, it did not convert the unconverted.
But neither did the Popular Television Association, despite

its membership claims and its avalanche of publicity, effect more than a simulation of public interest and activity.

What, then, did these two organizations finally achieve? There is little doubt that the National Television Council was effective in crystallizing already existing opposition to commercial television, thereby giving it a more powerful voice. It is probable that the pressure exerted by this group was crucial in blocking any attempt to introduce complete sponsorship on American lines.* It is also likely that its influence was important in the eventual creation of a public authority to own the transmitting facilities and licence the programme companies, and in the inclusion of many of the safeguards in the final Independent Television Act.

Probably the most important result of the work of the Popular Television Association was its ability to convince the Government and hesitant Conservative M.P.s that, although the general public was not overly excited about commercial television, there would at least be no disastrous electoral result from its introduction. While it was probably true that the majority of Conservative voters were opposed to commercial television (in contrast, ironically, to the majority of Labour voters, who favoured it)† the more important fact was demonstrated that the majority of owners and potential owners of television sets were more interested in a second channel than in the means by which it was obtained.

* Proponents of commercial television were actually split on this issue; there were a number of "moderates" who were also opposed to direct sponsorship.

† In the *News Chronicle*, June 23, 1953, Randolph Churchill commented that "It appears that the rank and file of the Tory Party are more intelligent than their M.P.s, whereas the rank and file of the Labour Party lack the enlightenment of theirs." And Labour M.P. Richard Crossman later observed, "In my experience the strongest opposition comes from non-viewing Conservatives whereas Labour supporters who view regularly are chiefly concerned to have as many programmes to select from as possible." (*Sunday Pictorial*, August 8, 1954.)

CHAPTER VIII

THE FINAL PHASE

LOOKING BACK ON events after July 2, 1953, when the Government's announcement of a forthcoming White Paper on television policy seemed to herald a retreat, it becomes obvious that by August 29th the chance to defeat commercial television had ended. On that day, at Mottram, Cheshire, Lord De La Warr, the Postmaster-General, made a statement which, while it reflected the Cabinet's concern for the misgivings that had been expressed by "thoughtful and serious people," represented a final capitulation to the Conservative backbenchers. It assured the critics within the Conservative Party that the forthcoming plan would not include "the American system of dependence on what is known as sponsoring" and that the BBC would remain unaltered. The Government merely wanted to provide alternative programmes because it distrusted monopoly "from however good a source it may come" and the only practical way of financing these programmes was through advertising.

There is little doubt that the original intention had been to introduce commercial television with sponsored programmes. This had been officially declared by the Lord Chancellor in May, 1952, and was still reflected in the speeches of Conservative M.P.s during the summer of 1953.[1] According to some of those involved in the intraparty controversy, the Government had been warned early in

July, 1953, by the Government Whip in the Lords, that if the Commons accepted any plan for sponsored television it would be defeated in the House of Lords. It was at this time, in the view of some, that Mr. R. A. Butler advised dropping the original scheme and bringing in the compromise measure suggested by the Postmaster-General and described by the second Conservative White Paper.

In July it had been generally thought that a number of influential Ministers were seriously disturbed by the weight and authority of the opposition to commercial television.* Several apparently regretted the Government's commitment and wanted to move very slowly, for this, they felt, was certainly not an issue of Conservative principle or of Party dogma. At the same time, probably a majority of back-benchers had finally accepted the brief of the Broadcasting Group stating the ideological argument against monopoly, and charging that the BBC was somewhat "pink", that it could never attract men of the highest artistic, scientific or administrative ability, and that in certain circumstances it would be an instrument of political indoctrination. They were indifferent to any argument based on the vulgarity of American commercial broadcasting, or the possibility of lowering standards in Britain. On the other hand, there were still a considerable number of Conservative M.P.s who were hostile to commercial television, or uncertain about the political

* An editorial, "Commercial Television", in the *Sunday Times*, July 5, 1953, expressed a common reaction. "The cautious tone of the Government's statement on commercial television last week appears to stem from a belated recognition that there is a very large body of opinion in the country, not least among Conservative supporters, that is strongly opposed to television or radio advertising, or at the lowest has grave doubts of the wisdom of launching a policy so difficult to revoke, until the case for it has been far more overwhelmingly proven. In terms merely of political expediency, to rush ahead might cost the Government many votes."

desirability of forcing the issue.* They were buttonholed by
convinced and persuasive Members and urged to go along to
avoid giving the appearance of Party disunity.

After the bitter outbursts among Conservative backbenchers during the presentation on July 2nd of the Government's vague statement on television, which they interpreted
as a deliberate delay of any action, even those Ministers who
were determinedly anti-commercial hesitated to provoke their
Members further. They were aware, as one commentator
observed, that "political realists would be unwise to under-
estimate the bitterness of the quarrel inside the Tory Party
over sponsored television. Lifelong friends are in some cases
scarcely on speaking terms. . . ."²

The Government was faced with a difficult dilemma. For
the Cabinet to have repudiated its commitment to introduce
"some element of competition" at this stage, would have
appeared as a capitulation to the Opposition. In the circumstances it was advisable to move cautiously, seeking a
compromise while reassuring their irate Members of the
Government's intention to introduce competitive television.
This was the substance of Mr. R. A. Butler's agreement with
the 1922 Committee on July 9th. Two weeks later the

* The uncertainty expressed in this letter to a constituent is not
unrepresentative of the feelings of many Conservative M.P.s: "I
am rather hoping that time will be allowed for second thoughts on
this [sponsored television] and that the Government will not
proceed in pushing through as a Party measure what is essentially
a controversial matter. As far as I am concerned, it is a subject on
which I have a completely open mind. I see the dangers clearly of a
BBC monopoly, especially in the political field, and I also see the
dangers of vulgarity and a lowering of the standards creep in if
commercial television is introduced and allowed a free hand.

"On balance, I think I would tend to oppose the Government's
proposals unless any convincing new arguments were brought, but
I could not undertake to help in the overthrow of the Government
by voting against it in the division lobby, in view of the quite
remarkable salvage work being undertaken in most other ways."

Conservative Radio & Television Committee decided to take every possible means to hold the Government to this commitment by taking their case against the monopoly of the BBC to the constituencies in the weeks before the Conservative Party Conference at Margate.

The change in the climate from June and July, when all but a handful of the most devout advocates were convinced that their cause was lost, was primarily due to the intensive work of some Conservative backbenchers, the Radio & Television Committee, the Popular Television Association, and the professional staff at the Conservative Central Office. As mentioned earlier, it was probably the case at this time that a majority of Conservative voters favoured the BBC and were certainly hostile to advertising either on radio or on television. * Thus proponents of commercial television had to overcome the antipathy of many Conservative supporters and convince the Government that votes would not be lost. Conservative M.P.s held meetings and Press conferences in their constituencies to convince supporters that an alternative to the BBC was a party issue and that the Party was advocating sponsored television because it was against monopoly.† They offered assurances that nothing would be done to harm the BBC and that British sponsored television would not be anything like that in the United States. There would be controls and, in any case, British taste was superior to the American and would never tolerate abuses.‡

* Even Lady Tweedsmuir, M.P., one of the original backbench group, said: "I myself, do not like advertisements on television, although I favour commercial television in this country. This may sound illogical, but I think the advantages gained will outweigh the disadvantages." (*Aberdeen Bon Accord*, September 17, 1953.)

† It is of interest that most of the M.P.s supporting an alternative system took it for granted, as judged by their speeches during the summer of 1953, that it would be sponsored television with advertisers providing the programmes.

‡ One M.P. hopefully suggested that "We might even do something to improve the American taste in this matter."

A reported speech by Sir David Eccles at the Purton Conservative féte in September is typical of many given during the campaign to win support of Conservative voters. "The BBC knows its own standards are pretty low and is frightened of competition. I have no doubt that we ought not to leave such a powerful instrument of control over people's thinking and their information in the hands of a Government monopoly. You would not like it if you had only one newspaper. The opposition to some form of competition in television is sponsored by people who will lose money—the present advertising revenue-getters, the newspapers. I do not blame them. Anyone interested in the great principles of liberty should reflect that the dictators—Stalin, Hitler, Mussolini, Franco—would have been against alternative television programmes. . . . You should think twice before you support something the great dictators were certain to favour. It is grossly unfair on British businessmen and the great firms of this country to say that they would have the same level of advertisements and behave in the same way as firms outside this country. Our big firms show great restraint and good taste. Our advertising is not vulgar."[3]

In conducting an intensive propaganda campaign during these months, the Conservative Central Office worked closely with and through its satellite organization the Popular Television Association. This, despite the fact that the Government had apparently instructed Central Office and Ministers not to participate in open controversy on this issue.* So intimate was the relationship in fact, that it is difficult to tell where one left off and the other began. The Central Office staff provided speakers with a detailed brief

* "The Government would not allow the Central Office, or its Ministers, to refute the many misrepresentations which were being spread about during this campaign. They let it build up until the Government was in such a position that it could do nothing except back down." (Backbench memorandum, "Television: Some Notes on the Government's White Paper" [Cmd. 9005] November 18, 1953.)

outlining the case for commercial television. Whatever the
particular organization label for speaker or pamphlet, the
arguments presented were identical. One of the most successful productions of Mr. Mark Chapman-Walker was the
persuasive but controversial leaflet "There's Free Speech!
Why Not Free Switch?", which carried the Central Office
label. Opponents of "competitive" television were listed as
the Labour Party, "unvarying opponents of free enterprise
and freedom of choice"; the Monopolists, "those who have a
vested interest in maintaining the monopoly of the BBC";
and the "Moral" Critics, who dislike television and think it
best to hold up the march of progress. This classification
hardly satisfied the most authoritative and distinguished
opponents of commercial television. The hostile reception
accorded this publication by many Conservatives and by
Conservative newspapers demonstrated the advantages of
having a nominally independent organization like the Popular
Television Association conduct controversial campaigns.
The *Sunday Times* thought it "regrettable that the party
alignment has been stiffened by publication of a frankly
propagandistic broadsheet in favour of commercial television
by the Conservative Central Office"[4] and the *Daily Mail*
referred to it as "the recent ill-considered television leaflet." *
This kind of reaction may have influenced the decision to have
all subsequent publications issued in the name of the Popular
Television Association.

* August 12, 1953. The Westminster columnist for *Truth*
observed: "The pamphlet is an efficient piece of propaganda—as
most Tory Central Office publications are—but I can't help wonder-
ing what is going to be said the next time the Tory high-ups
assemble in council. For the Party is badly divided on the issue of
competitive television, and some very influential supporters of the
Party—Lord Halifax, for example—are not likely to be overjoyed at
being lumped together in the pamphlet as 'The Moral Critics' and
told that they do not know all the facts and that their case is much
exaggerated." (August 7, 1953.)

Whatever the impact on the general public, this campaign by the Central Office and the Popular Television Association was obviously effective with the delegates to the Party Conference at Margate in October. In effect the Postmaster-General's statement at Mottram was overwhelmingly ratified by the Conference.* Of five accepted resolutions dealing with television, four supported the Government's policy, while the fifth merely requested a free vote in the House The managers of the Conference arranged for limited debate, with four topics including television scheduled between 2.30 and 5 p.m. Sir Robert Grimston, a leading proponent of commercial television and vice-chairman of the Party's Radio & Television Committee, warned that the State monopoly of broadcasting was a step on the slippery slope of totalitarianism. Grimston was not in favour of a free vote on what he considered a "fundamental principle of Conservative policy." Mr. Walter Elliott made the most effective appeal to the delegates when he cleverly tied up the question of commercial television with the misleading charge that "Mr. Morgan Phillips [Secretary of the Labour Party] had vetoed the televising of the Conservative Conference. His [Mr. Phillips'] decision, followed by that

* The *Manchester Guardian* reported that there were only five dissentients in the Winter Gardens where the main body of the conference met and as little opposition in the overflow meeting at the Lido Theatre. (October 9, 1953.) This result may merely reflect what Robert McKenzie has called "the traditionally deferential attitude of the rank and file." He notes the fact that "since 1945 all but three or four of the resolutions before each conference have been carried unanimously and increasingly of late the conference has tended to serve primarily as a demonstration of party solidarity and of enthusiasm for its own leaders." (R. T. McKenzie, *British Political Parties*, London: William Heinemann Ltd., 1955, pp. 198 & 189.) The unanimity of the conference may have had a further effect, for on November 16, 1953 the *News Chronicle* reported that there had been a 13 per cent swing among Conservative voters in favour of television advertising.

of the BBC, had provided a working model of a State monopoly."[5] The facts are that on July 17, 1953, the BBC wrote
in identical terms to the Conservative Party and the Labour
Party asking for their views on the proposal to televise the
Conferences. The Conservative Party replied that it would
need to consult the National Union of Conservative and
Unionist Associations. The Labour Party replied that as it
was a matter on which the Conference itself would have to
be consulted, it was decided not to accept the proposal for
that year (1953). The Conservative Party was informed of
the Labour Party's decision, and replied that the National
Union would consider "in due course" the question of
whether the Conference should be televised in future years—
it being assumed that there could be no question of its being
televised in that year. In all discussions of the subject since
Mr. Chapman-Walker first made the suggestion in a letter
to the BBC on July 15, 1952, the assumption was that the
BBC must televise both Conferences or neither. There is no
doubt that this was understood by the Parties. Conceivably
the opposition vote in the Conference might have been
greater had the anti-commercial case been presented with
some competence, or had the delegates not accepted television as a party political issue.* After this stage in the
controversy only the House of Lords could have defeated the
Government's plan.

Outside the Party, moderates among commercial pro-
ponents had reacted favourably to the Postmaster-General's
preview of the Government's plan for commercial television
without sponsoring. The pamphlet "Open Letter to the
Postmaster-General", which was produced by the Ducker
Committee on September 23, 1953, and signed by Mr.
P. G. E. Warburton, President of the Incorporated Society of
British Advertisers, and by Mr. Hubert Oughton, President

* One of the opposition speakers, a cinema-owner, was opposed
to any extension of television: this free entertainment which was,
he said, analagous to the State providing free beer!

of the Institute of Incorporated Practitioners in Advertising, expressed appreciation for the "very clear statement" defining the framework in which commercial television would operate. Mr. Norman Collins was reported satisfied, commenting that "the Government seem to have adopted the suggestion which was made in a booklet published several months ago by advertisers. . . ."[6] And at its autumn conference, October 1st, the Association of British Chambers of Commerce rejected the principle of sponsored programmes, declaring in favour of alternative stations presenting programmes in which commercial publicity could appear.[7]

On November 13, 1953, the Postmaster-General presented to Parliament the Government's *Memorandum on Television Policy*.[8] Two factors influenced what the White Paper characterized as "a typically British approach to this new problem": technical considerations and the concern that programme standards should not be lowered. Shortages of frequencies meant that only one network could be set up immediately, and cost considerations ruled out the feasibility of having a series of local independent stations. Therefore the Government proposed the establishment of a public corporation which would own and operate the transmitting stations, renting these facilities to private programme-producing companies who would sell time to advertisers. Consultation with the advertising bodies had led to the conclusion that separating advertisers from programme control would not jeopardize the financial success of the new system. As a basic principle, therefore, there was to be no sponsoring—"the responsibility for what goes out on the air shall rest with the operator of the station and not on the advertiser." It was felt that by combining the controlling authority with the actual ownership of the transmitting facilities, the authority's capacity to maintain standards would be strengthened. To reassure advertisers and those who feared "government control" these would normally be reserve powers. "In practice," the White Paper stated, "the fewer rules and less day-to-day interference the better; the need would be for a continuing friendly and constructive contact between the corporation and the companies." Control over the amount of broadcasting by the new system, as with the BBC, remained with the Postmaster-General.

The White Paper was generally recognized as a compromise that hardly satisfied anyone, but that might get the Government out of trouble.* For those who feared the deterioration of broadcasting standards, the major flaw was the complete dependence of the new system on revenue from advertising. There was also doubt that sponsoring had really been avoided, since it was believed advertisers would certainly select programmes with mass appeal.† Censorship by the authority, it was felt, could not produce high standards, but only operate negatively to prevent gross breaches of minimum standards.

* "The Government's White Paper on sponsored television offers an ingenious solution, which may get them out of a deal of trouble." (*Financial Times*, November 16, 1953. See also *The Times Educational Supplement*, November 20, 1953.)

† Jack Gould, radio critic for the *New York Times*, commented on this difficulty "Last week's proposal of the Conservative Party to set up within a year or so a video service that would enjoy all the fruits of advertising and none of the drawbacks is a naïve hope unlikely to survive practical experience. . . . In the United States the placement of the 'spot' announcement, such as the British propose to adopt exclusively, is an inordinately complicated and tricky business itself. The real goal of the advertiser is to get his 'spot' bang up next to a top show at a peak listening period. When and where the 'spot' is put not alone determines its cost, but may determine the quality of the adjacent program.

"If the broadcaster were to put on readings of Shakespeare by a college professor, he could be sure that he would not attract many 'spot' announcements. But if he put on a couple of give-aways or a popular disc-jockey show, 'spot' business would boom. Would the fate of the Bard be in doubt?" (November 22, 1953.)

Within the advertising industry reception was mixed. An editorial in *World's Press News*, "TV without Trust", expressed the view of many agents: "Well, it looks as if they are going to give us a second television service—grudgingly. Of course the wicked advertisers will be thoroughly controlled, they will be closely watched, nobody will trust them further than they can see—if as far. What an old-fashioned anti-social idea it was that the man who paid the piper called the tune."[9] Mr. A. O. Buckingham, head of Young & Rubicam, was equally bitter at what he called a milk and water approach that put "the strongest selling medium that has yet been devised" in a strait-jacket. "This is not competitive TV. This is a miniscule BBC operating under handicaps which even that august body has never had to face."[10] A former president of the Glasgow Chamber of Commerce expressed doubts as to the value of advertising if it were not directly associated with particular programmes. Others considered that the ban on sponsoring was a backward step which would jeopardize the financial support of the new system.[11] In contrast, a columnist in *Advertisers' Weekly* insisted that "organized advertising is happy because, broadly speaking, its recommendations have been accepted." This meant that the ISBA-IIPA committee under Cyrus Ducker "will stamp the future of competitive TV in this country. And that will be a lasting reminder of the part played by advertising in the establishment of a public service."*

* November 19, 1953. An editorial in *Broadcasting*, leading trade organ of American radio and television broadcasters, said: "You'll pardon us, old chappies, if we snicker a bit over the White Paper issued by Her Majesty's Government proclaiming that Britain will have commercial television. But, says the paper, 'it will bear no resemblance to the American system'. . . .

"We submit, one can't be just a 'little bit' commercial. Either it is or it isn't.

"The restrictions they propose to throw about the new

Following more than a year of discussion in Press and Parliament it was apparent to all that no new arguments would be developed during the course of the White Paper debate in the House of Lords (November 25-26) or in Commons (December 14-15, 1953). These occasions did, however, reveal the pressures on the Government from anti-commercial forces, and from its own backbenchers who bitterly resented both what they considered the Government's dilatory tactics and its sensitivity to Establishment opinion.

Initially the debate in the House of Lords was to have taken place on a motion by Lord Reith, which merely called attention to the White Paper without forcing a Division. Lord Reith agreed to withdraw his motion and in its place there was tabled on November 18th a motion by Lord Halifax:

"Whilst recognizing the desirability of an alternative television programme, this House regrets that it cannot approve the proposals of Her Majesty's Government as outlined in the memorandum on television policy."

Cabinet Ministers were reported to have been disturbed by this switch in opposition plans because, when they had decided on November 17th to delay debate in Commons until after the Lords had discussed the matter, they had thought that debate would occur on Lord Reith's innocuous motion. It was suggested that this change led to the decision to issue a

---

commercial operations would make our wildest-eyed rigid regulationists cringe.

"So, as we sail away from the chalk walls, bleak cliffs (or whatever they are) of the tight little British Isles, we say:

> Dear little John Bulls,
> Don't you cry;
> You'll be full commercial
> Bye and bye."

two-line Whip, normally issued to peers who support the Government when their presence is required. Lord Salisbury, Conservative leader in Lords, sent an official message to Government peers that their attendance "throughout both days of this important debate, so far as possible, is earnestly requested, but your Lordship is asked most particularly to be in your place not later than 4 p.m. on Thursday, November 26th, to support the Government in the Division. . . ."[12]

The Times perhaps underestimated the Government's sense of urgency in stating that "the two-line whip issued by the Government for this debate suggests that future television policy is not regarded as an issue of the first significance and that a moderately urgent summons to Government peers will bring up enough of them to defeat Lord Halifax and the peers of all parties who are to support his motion, if this is pressed to a division."* Neither the Labour Party nor the Liberal Party issued a Whip, although in the debate Lord Salisbury referred to a letter, sent to all peers in the name of Lord Halifax, as being equal to a Party Whip.[13] At a meeting of the National Television Council on November 18th, it had been proposed that a letter be sent to Members of the House of Lords asking them to attend the debate and support the Motion. Lord Halifax had telegraphed his consent and the letter was sent out by the Council to several hundred peers on November 21st. It seems unlikely that Lord Salisbury was entirely candid in implying that his Whip was merely a reaction to the Halifax letter. The fact is, as Mr. P. A. Bromhead has noted, that the Government, "full of apprehension lest the voting should go against its policy, took great pains to ensure that there would be a big attendance of amenable peers. These precautions were clearly necessary."[14]

---

* November 21, 1953. According to Lord Salisbury, "the Whip . . . in this House, at any rate, is not an order. It is an indication of the way the Government would like its supporters to vote." (H.L. Debs. 184:741.)

The debate attracted the largest attendance in the House of Lords for many years.* Passions were high and many tempers frayed before the debate concluded.† In the end, the Government defeated the Halifax motion by a majority of 70, but there were 87 votes against the policy and, if estimates are correct that there were very nearly 350 Conservative peers present in the House, over 100 abstained from voting. Actually, the Government may have been reasonably satisfied with the result in view of the Whip's earlier forecast of defeat.

There is the likelihood that the vehement debate in the Lords strengthened the Government's determination to go on with their compromise measure. This may have been the unintended contribution of Lord Hailsham, whose passion bordering on hysteria and angry outburst at the close of the debate offended Members who might otherwise have voted against the Government. Because of an attack of influenza, Lord Halifax was unable to speak on behalf of his

* Bromhead, op. cit. p. 32: "In the past thirty years only two purely political questions have produced divisions with over 200 peers voting—a series of divisions on the Commons' rejection of Lords amendments to the Coal Mines Bill in 1930, and plans for Indian constitutional reform in 1934 and 1935. On the other hand, a bill to allow peeresses to sit in the House brought out 206 peers to vote in 1926, and over 200 voted on each of two other proposals for the reform of the House, in 1927 and 1933; 216 peers voted on the liquor control bill in 1924, and 289 on the Prayer Book question in 1927. Coming down to more recent times, we find 258 and 238 peers voting on the two second readings of the Parliament Bill in 1948, 244 on a motion condemning independent television in 1953, 209 on the death penalty in 1948 and 333 on the same subject in 1956."

† The *Manchester Guardian*, on November 27, 1953, commented: "A political or economic issue on which the fate of the nation depended could hardly have provoked a controversy in which conflicting views were combined with such deep feeling." See also *The Statist*, December 4, 1953.

Motion. This meant that Lord Hailsham opened and closed the debate. Some observers were inclined to believe that had Lord Halifax been there to make a more temperate appeal and then withdrew the motion, the Government might have been more inclined to seek another solution, or at least accept an all-party conference. Never excessively popular with Sir Winston and some other Ministers, Lord Hailsham had not added to his appeal by attacking his own Party leadership for practising "shoddy, disreputable politics" in deliberately omitting from the Conservative election manifesto any reference to commercial television, or in accusing the Government of "disreputable public finance . . . fundamentally vicious and corrupting" in proposing that the new broadcasting public corporation be financed with a Treasury loan.[15] His listeners in the Lords' debate were hardly more enthusiastic when he attacked as "muddle-headedness" the Cabinet's effort to arrive at an acceptable solution. ". . . Inside the realm of some questions of principle," said Lord Hailsham, "compromise is not so much a typically British or admirable thing as a sort of intellectual smog—something which is a passport to chaos and confusion and a convenient cloak for complete muddle-headedness."*

In one of the ironies of politics the Government's most effective speaker was Lord Salisbury, then Lord President of the Council and leader of the House. Speaking on February

* H.L. Debs. 184:517-518. Lord Hailsham subsequently told the BBC Staff Association that submission of the TV Bill to Parliament was "a shoddy and squalid constitutional error," presumably because it had not been included in the Party election manifesto. (*Sunday Chronicle*, May 23, 1954.) He elaborated this point in the Lords' Second Reading debate, July 1, 1954: "This is a disreputable piece of chicanery, and it can be described in no other language. It is not simply the absence of a mandate; it is a deliberate concealment, so far as one can judge, of a vital element in a political programme, which either was, or ought to have been, well within the contemplation of the leaders of the Party at the time of the General Election." (H.L. Debs. 188:397.)

28, 1952, to the 1922 Committee, Lord Salisbury had sought to persuade the Parliamentary Party to support the Government's intention, which was at that time to renew the BBC Charter unchanged.[16] Now he was committed to defend, even advocate, a policy he was thought previously to have opposed.

For the final form the television bill was to take, the most important opposition contributions came from the Archbishop of Canterbury and Lord Waverley, president of the National Television Council.[17] Both made moderate speeches regretting that television had become a subject of party controversy and pleading that the Government seek an agreed solution to the issue. They urged in particular that the new system should not be financed solely by advertising revenue. The Archbishop, though he preferred no advertisements at all, suggested that if accepted they appear on both systems with revenue going to a common fund supporting both the BBC and the new system. Lord Waverley took a similar position in urging that the Government "look again at the finance and other features of their scheme with a view to getting rid of this . . . most undesirable feature of dependence upon advertisements."

In summing up, Lord Salisbury said that the Government had "never spoiled for a fight on this question," and indicated that the ideas suggested by the Archbishop and Lord Waverley were "worthy of further study."

There was little of this tone of reasonableness in the Commons debate. Mr. Herbert Morrison's request, supported by three Liberal Members, for an all-party conference was rejected by Mr. Selwyn Lloyd unless the Labour Party would accept the breaking of the BBC's monopoly and agree that the alternative system should draw its revenue from advertisements. Captain Gammans argued that the Opposition had made it a party issue by threatening to reverse any scheme of the Government.

Those Conservative M.P.s who had initiated the campaign

for commercial broadcasting were far from pleased with the
White Paper proposals, and disliked the moderate statements
in Lords of Lord Salisbury and the Postmaster-General. In
fact, Mr. Anthony Fell "found the White Paper to be
probably the most depressing document I have ever read in
my life."[18] He resented the fact that a public corporation was
to have "a flexible control" over the programme companies,
including the power to withdraw licences. There was strong
objection to the clause permitting the Postmaster-General to
specify the number of hours of broadcasting, for it was known
that the programme companies would want more time than
the BBC, since each additional hour increased the possibility
of obtaining advertising revenue. These backbenchers were
particularly incensed by any further delay, either as the result
of all-party talks, or by conferences with Conservative
opponents of the new scheme. Still believing "that the
Government was in no hurry to prove its firmness of purpose," the backbenchers were intensely concerned with
timing the introduction of the commercial system.[19]

In a memorandum on November 9th, Mr. Chapman-
Walker urged the importance of having commercial television a "working reality at the next General Election" and
stressed the dangers of further delay. He had been informed,
he wrote, that the first few months of television would be of
"spectacularly high quality. This of course is because the
commercial television operators will know that they are on
trial, and having had considerable warning of the advent of
television they will have been able to collect some excellent
programmes which they will concentrate into the opening
months, and therefore it is possible that the initial practice
of commercial television in this country may well overcome
even the opposition of the intellectuals and the ecclesiastics."
Furthermore, although "opposition still persists in some
quarters of our Party . . . this opposition is decreasing." In
addition, "recently there have been reports from our can-
vassers and workers in Socialist areas that they believe that

the introduction of competitive television will become a 'vote winner amongst our opponents'." The Labour Party would then "have to campaign on the basis of taking it away" and "we should have in our hands a major election issue which I have no doubt we could use to great advantage, and it might prove such a popular issue as to obliterate some of the other things we may not want to over-emphasize at the next General Election." With this in mind, he suggested a time-table scheduling commercial television to be on the air by July-August, 1955.[20]

Even this was not considered speedy enough by the back-bench proponents. They insisted that "all legislation should be cleared by the end of February, 1954, the Corporation should be given the green light by March, 1954, in which case the stations would start by March, 1955. It is even more urgent that the Radio Industry should be told what wave-lengths will be used, since otherwise there will be no sets capable of receiving the programmes when they start in March, 1955. Some feel that the Government must either get on with the proposal to break the monopoly, or it must drop the whole issue."*

Pressure on the Government to hold all-party discussions on its proposals continued after the White Paper debates. No formal discussions ever took place because the Government insisted that opponents must agree in advance that the BBC monopoly was to be ended and that advertising revenue would be the main source of finance for the new scheme.[21] While the Labour Party might have been willing to concede that a second programme should be independent of the BBC, they

---

* Backbench Memorandum, November 18, 1953. Provision of suitable sets proved to be no problem. The *Financial Times*, March 4, 1954, was able to report that set manufacturers "are well ahead with their plans to provide adapters to enable existing TV sets to receive competitive stations in Band III. . . ." and "Pye has had a multi-station (13 channel) set on retail sale throughout the country since mid-January."

would not accept the advertising provision.* However, the National Television Council conveyed to the Government their acute dissatisfaction with the scheme outlined in the White Paper. Their main objection was its financial dependence on advertising revenue which meant, they believed, that advertisers would control the programmes with a consequent lowering of standards. They feared as well that the anticipated substantial revenue for the commercial system would mean unfair competition that would undermine the BBC by taking away technicians, producers, and artists. It was also argued that the division of responsibility between the proposed Authority and the programme companies would make it impossible to enforce standards.

At a meeting of the Organizing Committee of the Council on January 19th, it was decided that Lord Waverley should make the necessary arrangements for a deputation to the Government. The result was a meeting on January 25th between Lady Violet Bonham Carter, Lord Waverley, Lord Beveridge and Mr. Christopher Mayhew representing the Council, and Lord Woolton, Lord De La Warr, Sir David Maxwell Fyfe, and Captain David Gammans for the Government.[22] Though many of the details of the plan were still vague, some assurance was apparently obtained that the proposed Authority would be strengthened against the programme companies. Specifically it was thought that the idea expressed in the White Paper, that the Authority should only intervene on special occasions, had been abandoned. Instead, powers would be exercised until experience justified relaxation of controls. In particular, the programme companies would be required to submit programmes and scripts to the Authority.

The trials and tribulations of the Government were not ended with the introduction of the Bill on March 4, 1954. For another five months the Government was knocked about

* "Might" because Mr. Herbert Morrison was opposed to any alternative to the BBC.

between opponents of commercial television and disgruntled advocates. The principal departure of the Bill from the White Paper scheme was a provision of public money for the proposed new corporation, the Independent Television Authority. As much as £750,000 was to be provided annually by Parliament on request of the Authority, and in addition the Postmaster-General, with Treasury consent, was authorized to loan the Authority up to £2,000,000. In other provisions the Bill was generally consistent with the policy outlined in the White Paper.

This provision of an annual grant, the only major concession to the opponents of commercial television, satisfied no one and outraged the backbench group. It had been introduced by the Government in an effort to meet the request of Lord Waverley and the Archbishop of Canterbury that the Authority not be completely dependent on advertising revenue.[23] For the opponents of a commercial system the annual grant represented an inadequate gesture that would not alter dependence on advertising revenue and which was interpreted as a subsidy for advertisers filched from the BBC.*

The Popular Television Association and their backbench allies were equally dissatisfied and more vehement in their condemnation of the Government's Bill. Mr. Ronald Simms characterized it as "a sorry compromise whose initial ideas have been lost in a maze of restrictions."[24] They had thought that the White Paper was "a first step in the right direction, and believed that it represented the limit of compromise." Now the Bill contained provisions "which strike not only at the freedom and hope of success of commercial television, but at the fundamental principles of democratic thought."[25] Captain L. P. S. Orr, the Group's principle spokesman in these debates, condemned both the provision of the annual grant and the fact that the Authority was to build the television transmitters.[26] In his judgment there was no need to

* *The Economist* more correctly termed it a "subsidy against advertisers." (March 6, 1954.)

have the Bill at all, for the Postmaster-General already had the authority to license commercial transmitters.[27] The general attitude of backbench proponents was expressed by Sir Herbert Williams (Croydon, East) in declaring that the Bill had not been welcomed because "the bulk of this Bill has been invented to placate a whole lot of sloppy-minded people who do not wish to get on with the job."[28] They objected both to the powers granted the new Authority and to what they considered its subservience to the Post Office—always a target of the broadcasting Group. In their opinion, the Bill discouraged potential programme contractors by permitting the Authority itself to produce programmes and by providing for pre-censorship of commercial programmes. Most serious, however, was the absence of security for the programme contractors. For this reason they wanted licences allocated on the basis of one company to one station.

Outside Parliament the Bill received an almost equally unenthusiastic reception. A radio industry trade journal observed that "Whatever the outcome of the debate . . . it is clear that neither our Industry nor those outside who had prepared to invest in TV advertising had any enthusiasm for the Government plan." It thought that had the industry known what it was to get it might have been better off to have worked for commercial television through the BBC transmitters.[29] A managing director of one programme company was quoted as saying that "The Bill is so bad that no amendments could put it right."[30] Sir Robert Renwick thought that many of the safeguards included in the Bill "must be deplored by true supporters of free enterprise." Nevertheless, "free enterprise may be taken as ready to co-operate, provided that the Authority does not in any circumstances become a programme planning or operating corporation."[31]

The advertising industry, while not unanimous, was pleased that the Bill "represents a triumph for a point of principle. At long last . . . a British Government has recognized that there is a place for advertising in the field of broadcasting. . . . The science of selling has established its right to a share in a medium which it has for too long, and quite unreasonably been denied."[32] *Advertisers' Weekly* was at least encouraged by what they considered the absence of restrictive legislation: that no attempt was made to lay down the number of contracts which the Authority must make with programme contractors, and that "as much as possible appears to have been left for negotiation" with the Authority. They were not satisfied with "the rather nebulous nature of the Bill . . . as regards magazine programmes, shopping guides, and the use of documentaries."[33] Mr. Ian Harvey, M.P. and a director of W. S. Crawford, Ltd., warned that the relegation of advertising "spots" in between programmes would not be satisfactory. "If the Government thinks that sort of thing would provide a workable proposition it will have to think again." For there should be, said Mr. Harvey, no objection to the introduction of advertising as "a natural part of the programme."[34]

Since the measure as introduced to Parliament was mainly an enabling Bill with its precise working out extremely vague, it was found to be very susceptible to amendment. During Committee stage in Commons 206 amendments were tabled, and the Government itself placed sixteen amendments on the Order Paper after the Bill was published. The Labour Opposition introduced 145 amendments designed, in their judgment at least, to clarify, to strengthen the Authority in its relation to programme contractors, to extend coverage to all sections of the country, to protect the interests of British actors and writers, and to prevent advertising on Sunday programmes. None of the Opposition amendments dealing with any of these issues were accepted by the Government. In fact, the Conservatives interpreted most of the amendments as "wrecking" amendments, an interpretation not unsupported by the statement of Miss Margaret Herbison (Lanarkshire, North) that "If we could get the Minister to accept every one of these Amendments, the Bill would in reality come to nought. (*Laughter.*) I say it quite openly."[35] After two days of debate on the first three subsections, including two hours arguing that "Commercial" should be substituted for "Independent" in the name of the Authority, Sir David Maxwell Fyfe justifiably introduced the Guillotine procedure. Even so, about eighty hours were spent in debate in the Commons.

Some Government amendments met the objections of those Conservative M.P.s who were still sceptical about commercial broadcasting and distrustful of efforts to weaken controls over advertisers and programme companies.* Thus, the Government slightly limited "give-away" programmes†;

* Mr. A. E. Cooper (Ilford, South), a spokesman for this group, was disturbed by statements of the Assistant Postmaster-General which seemed to imply increased advertising control. "Throughout the whole of the debates on this Bill, I have found it very hard to give support to my hon. and right hon. friends, although it is well known that certain of us on this side of the House have reservations about the merits of this Bill . . . I was somewhat astonished at the speech which my hon. friend the Assistant Postmaster-General made a few months ago. The whole burden of the reservations which some of us have made on this Bill has been on this precise question of advertiser control of the programmes, and, had it not been for the assurances which we have received over and over again and the safeguards, which we believe are adequate, which have been placed in the Bill, we would most certainly not have supported this Bill in its passage through this House. . . . I find it difficult to reconcile the words in various parts of the Bill with the speech which my hon. friend has just made." (H.C. Debs. 529:292-293, June 22, 1954.)

† The Government amendment dealt with "a prize or gift which is available only to persons receiving that programme or in relation to which any advantage is given to such persons." This meant that prizes could only be won, or gifts received, by people present at the time of the broadcast either as part of the programme or in the studio audience. "Give-away" programmes as now broadcast in commercial programmes were not barred under the Act.

advertising agents were not to be eligible to be directors of programme companies; and advisory committees were to be appointed to advise the Authority and programme contractors on religious, medical, and advertising questions. Throughout the final stages of debate repeated assurance was given that advertisers would not be able to influence the type of programme presented and that there would be no advertisements in the middle of programmes. *

However, as Popular Television's executive had predicted, "Only in the House can we now expect an easing of the regulations so drastically imposed under the terms of the Bill."[36] Thus, most of the amendments accepted by the Government from its backbenchers were designed to weaken or minimize the role of the Independent Television Authority, make the new scheme more attractive to advertisers, and lessen competition between the programme companies. Sir Robert Renwick had warned that the commercial interests would co-operate so long as the Authority did not become "a programme planning or operating corporation."[37] To prevent the creation of a "junior BBC" the Bill was amended to limit the power of the Authority to provide studios and permit it to provide programmes itself only in exceptional and temporary circumstances. Captain L. P. S. Orr explained that "We have changed certain provisions to make it clear that the Authority is not to become another BBC. We had great fears about the Bill at first, and I personally had a lot of

* See, for example, H.L. Debs. 184:530, the Postmaster-General: "Needless to say, at no time would interruption of programmes be permitted." Also, Lord Fairfax: "Advertisements in the middle can be very annoying. However . . . that is not to be allowed over here. . . ." (Ibid. 630) and Lord Teynham: "The idea that advertisements would be inserted in the middle of a programme I am sure would be avoided in this country, as I am certain it would not be acceptable to the public." (Ibid. 657.) Also see H.C. Debs. 522:56, Mr. Gammans: "We do not propose to allow interruptions of programme with advertising material."

reservations on Second Reading. We feared that it would
allow the Authority . . . to own studios, to build a whole
empire for itself, and, in effect, in the end to reduce the
programme contractor to the position which a BBC producer
holds. . . . We have succeeded in getting that position right,
and it is now quite clear that if the Authority is ever to set up
studios it will be done only in the case of emergency.''[38] To
safeguard manufacturers the Authority was forbidden to
produce or sell equipment. In an effort to strengthen the
programme contractors, amendments were made limiting
the powers of the Authority to penalize them only if a
specific breach of contract was apprehended To the advantage of programme companies, advertising agents and advertisers, the Bill was amended to enable tariffs on advertisements to be raised when they accompanied programmes
specially attractive to advertisers, e.g. special events, or the
appearance of a celebrity. Many feared this change as likely
to enhance advertising control over the type of programmes
presented. Backbench suspicion of the Post Office was
reflected in a number of changes—narrowing the description
of items that the Government could request the Independent
Television Authority to broadcast; permitting the ITA when
broadcasting a requested item to announce that fact; requiring that the Postmaster-General formally notify Parliament
with regard to establishing additional stations or dismissing
a member of the Authority.

There were few significant changes made in the House of
Lords. They did increase the maximum penalty for breach
of contract by a programme company, widen the require-
ment that programmes be predominantly British by providing
that a proper proportion be of British performance, and add an
advisory committee on children's programmes. An Opposition amendment giving the Postmaster-General power to
specify the hours of the day in which the Authority could
broadcast was reluctantly accepted by the Government.
Though this was disliked by the commercial proponents in

the Commons, the Chairman of the Parliamentary broadcasting committee warned of the risk involved to the timetable if they attempted an alteration of this amendment.[39]

With the Whips on and an adequate Government majority, there never was any doubt that the Bill and its amendments would be approved, despite the lack of enthusiasm among both those M.P.s who first conceived the plan for commercial television and those who all along had reservations.* On July 30, 1954, after twenty days of debate and bargaining spread over five months, the Bill to create the Independent Television Authority became law.

* The vote on the Second Reading of the Bill was 296 to 269. (H.C. Debs. 525:1556.) As *The Economist* noted, on April 3, 1954, "Some of the least tractable [M.P.s] are threatening real trouble, but there is a saying among Tories these rebellious days: 'Your constituency or your conscience.' Whoever coined the phrase has so far proved an accurate if cynical judge of the pressures on this pressure group."

CHAPTER IX

SPECULATIONS

CAUTION IS CERTAINLY warranted in drawing conclusions from the legislative history of a single act. Obviously one is not justified in attempting to spin out an elaborate theory of pressure group politics. At the same time this one case study does support a degree of scepticism toward some of the generalizations which have been made about the operation of pressure groups and political parties in Britain. At the least one may conclude that to base the study of politics on the annual reports and published statements of the various organizations, groups or parties, may produce somewhat formal, even misleading, accounts of what is inevitably a dynamic and subtle process.

Despite diligent efforts to fill in details of the origins of the Independent Television Act, one is left with many questions unanswered, perhaps never to be answered unless future memoirs prove more richly informative than the current productions. Though one can list certain explanatory factors it is not easy, for example, to understand the procrastination of the Labour Government in renewing the BBC Charter after the Beveridge Committee had reported, or to explain Mr. Morrison's frequent lapses into dilatory inertia. One may suggest that the Labour leadership never fully comprehended the stakes involved in maintaining public service broadcasting. Was this a reflection of a general

Labour failure to grasp the more subtle implications of the commercialized mass media? Does the behaviour of the Labour Government, its lack of any sense of urgency, also illustrate its want of communication, of social intercourse with its Conservative opponents? Certainly there is evidence to suggest that Labour leadership consistently underestimated the quality, skill, energy and determination of those who reorganized and revitalized the Conservative Party after 1946. *

Perhaps, too, those who supported public service broadcasting and the BBC erred in counting too heavily on "the weight of authority", on the influence of the prominent and prestigeful, and thus failed to make more effective use of their more humble supporters. It is curious that so little was done to offset the stream of criticism inspired by the commercial advocates. Surely it should have been possible for the anti-commercial forces, many of them loyal and active Conservatives, to have been heard in constituency meetings and Party Conference. Though the Labour Party has built-in disadvantages for acquiring information informally, many of the BBC supporters might have been expected to know more about the organized nature of the commercial lobby. Is it possible that they underestimated the extent of latent popular hostility to some aspects of the BBC? There probably was a clear majority for the conception of public service broadcasting, but there was also in all parties and sections of the community some dislike for what was thought to be BBC authoritarianism or paternalism. Admittedly, these

* Lord Woolton comments in his *Memoirs*: "Mr. Morrison was fortified by a low opinion of me as a political organizer. On 1st July, 1946, he said about my appointment as Chairman of the Conservative Party, 'Knowing him as I do, it is O.K. by the Labour Party, and suits us down to the ground.' I always sought to support him in this view by assuring him that in the organization of Transport House the Socialist Party had an election machine without parallel." pp. 352-353.

aspects are of secondary importance, for it is conceivable that nothing done by either the Labour Government or the proponents of public service broadcasting could have done more than delay the aspirations of those working within the Conservative coalition who consider broadcasting to be primarily a commercial instrument.

This study would seem to establish the fact that a small number of M.P.s, well organized, with good connections among both Party officials and outside interests, and pushing a definite, limited programme, may exert considerable influence and even overwhelm an unorganized majority in their own party. If this be true it gives rise a to number of questions: Is it possible that the relation of M.P.s to outside interests needs further examination and clarification? The formal declaration of interest seems to have been neither inhibiting nor significant in this instance. In furthering the Television Act the outside interests seem to have exerted more effective influence than Conservative voters, constituency organizations, or even members of the Parliamentary Party. Obviously they had "established access to friendly M.P.s" and were certainly able to participate in initiating this legislation. One is less certain than Professor Finer that, in this case at least, Parliament "itself acts as a counter-check on any one lobby."[1] Here surely the "pitiless floodlight" which is supposed to be focused by a zealous opposition did not serve to limit the effectiveness of the outside interests.

One is also left with reservations about several aspects of Conservative Party organization and operation. In particular, the relations between the Party Leader and the Party Chairman, and between the Parliamentary Party and the professionals, need to be clarified. Robert McKenzie, in his authoritative study of British Parties, notes that "It is difficult to attempt a definite assessment of the power and authority of the Chairman in the councils of the party since obviously most of his influence is exerted behind the scenes."[2] In this particular case it would appear that the Chairman was something more than the agent of the Leader. In his *Memoirs* Lord Woolton quotes with approval a *Times* leader appraising his role: "He is not merely the maker of the machine: he has also exercised an influence greater than that of any of his predecessors among the Party's organizers on the making of policy."[3] He also suggests that Sir Winston was never very much interested in party organization and implies that he had "very little regard for the Conservative Central Office."[4] Whatever the complexities involved, the campaign for commercial television would appear to challenge the notion that the professionals never threaten "to become the real centre of power within" the party organization.[*] The evidence suggests that the Central Office professionals did operate to force the Party into more extreme positions. This could not have been accomplished without the approval and active support of the Chairman; whether he was acting under instructions and with the approval of the Leader we do not know. This experience suggests that it might be desirable to reconsider the relation between the Central Office and the mass organization of the Party, an issue entirely ignored in the Maxwell Fyfe Report on party organization.[5]

The impression is unavoidable that the professionals in the Central Office held the Party rank-and-file in low esteem. Prior to the Party Conference in October, 1953, there was active opposition to the introduction of commercial television among Conservatives. Representative of this sentiment is the criticism of the leaflet "There's Free Speech—Why Not Free Switch", in a monthly newsletter published by one Young Conservative Branch:

"Surely the propagation of the argument that there should be an additional sponsored TV network is very much a

* McKenzie, op. cit. p. 591. However, he notes that "The party bureaucracy, responsible only to the Leader of the Party, is just as fully in control of the affairs of the party as it was in the heyday of Captain Middleton sixty years ago." p. 291.

matter for the few big business concerns who stand to gain by it, and who presumably believe in it. It is very difficult to see why Central Office should spend the Party Funds on propaganda for independent business firms. And according to the Gallup Poll, three out of five Conservatives do *not* want commercial television. Did Central Office take this into account? It doesn't look like it!" "There is another curious aspect to this campaign. The Secretary of the 'P(opular) T(elevision) A(ssociation)' wrote an article recently for the *Recorder* setting out the argument for commercial TV. It was a somewhat novel argument, and on comparing it with the Central Office leaflet, there proved to be a remarkable similarity between the two. It seems as though, deliberately or by coincidence, the C(entral) O(ffice) leaflet is doing a propaganda job for the advertisers at the expense of the Party Funds."[6]

Yet in the reports of public opinion issued by the Central Office to constituency agents it was stressed that the general public was indifferent to the issue and that open criticism by Party members would be suppressed by loyalty once the Party line had been declared. The whole campaign reflects the public relations stress on manipulation, on the use of "gimmicks", to sell a pre-packaged policy. Thus the great play on "monopoly", the discreet substitution of "independent" for "commercial", and the emphasis on a hypothetical danger of partisan control of the BBC, although even Sir David Maxwell Fyfe emphasized in the final debate that "Everyone inside and outside this country knows of its (the BBC's) independence. . . . The point I am making is that the BBC is independent, is known to be independent and has a 30 years' tradition of independence."[7]

This case also raises some questions regarding McKenzie's contention that "neither party in office has sacrificed its conception of the national interest in order to serve the purposes of those sections of the community which provide its funds."[8] At least a degree of doubt is produced when one considers that a Government responsible for the introduction of commercial television (which at that time could only have resulted in increasing domestic demand and consumption), simultaneously ordered all departments to cut down their expenditures on the ground that Britain's economic problems were due to excessive domestic consumption and a slighting of the export market.

Though some Conservatives "dislike the vulgarity inherent in sponsored broadcasts"[9] others, including the Party professionals and presumably Lord Woolton, were aware of the likelihood that the direct influence of commercial broadcasting would redound to the benefit of the Conservative Party. Mr. Charles Orr-Ewing, in supporting commercial television, had written in 1953 that "The advantage should lie with the Conservative Party, because the more vulnerable Labour voters will be exposed to a new form of persuasion."[10] Lord Woolton may have had this in mind when he observed that "it seems to me to be dangerous to public morale that advertising should be regarded with cynical suspicion."[11]

Advertising inevitably establishes values, conceptions of the good life; but it is not merely the direct influence of the advertising message itself that is important, but the whole tone of programme content and orientation. The tendency of commercially sponsored programmes is to convey the notion, with varying degrees of subtlety, that there are no serious problems. They constitute the provision of "free" circuses on a vast scale. To this extent the delegate at the Party Conference in 1953 was not far wrong in likening commercial television to "free beer". A writer in *Crossbow* has stated that "Because the Conservative Party is so largely identified with the *status quo*, it cannot help but be benefited, indirectly and almost accidentally, by the insistent presentation to the electorate of stories and programmes which in one way or another make the point: 'Things are going fine',

'There's nothing to complain about' or 'If you have problems, change yourself, not society.' The Labour Party
suffers because it requires a widespread sense of social
discontent to gain more voters. The media are largely
uninterested in social problems, except as they concern Irish
horses and quick-fed calves, neither of which has the vote."[12]
In this sense the political significance of commercial television must be evaluated in conjunction with other Conservative policies, such as reduced restrictions on hire purchase,
lower down payments on homes, and the encouragement of
stock ownership, designed to produce "a property-owning
democracy."[13]

For these reasons, among others, it is perhaps misleading
to conclude that television is barred off to political advertising.[14] Technically this is true, but it may well be that the
daily fare of commercial television is more significant in the
formation of attitudes than is the overt propaganda of a
political campaign. This possibility was stressed by a Party
official to a group of Area Organization Leaders at Swinton
College in 1959. According to his interpretation, commercial
television has "done us incalculable good". It has brought
goods into people's homes and focused their attention on
them, raising their level of expectation. This in turn has
served to give people a stake in things, making them
conservative. In addition it has provided distraction, directing
desires and imaginations toward the products advertised.
Professor Otto Kirchheimer has argued that "The rise of
consumer-oriented public opinion formation has been one of
the most powerful elements in the reduction of the political
element to the semi-entertainment level."[15] Thus it is less
clear that disparity in financial resources between the parties
is insignificant. Mr. Finer, focusing on overt propaganda
between elections, concludes that the greater expenditure by
the Conservative coalition "would only prove significant if
the two most effective mass media, sound and vision, went
up to public auction. . . . As long as they are statutorily

neutralized, as they are, the propaganda effects of wealth are not very substantial."[16] This is to take a narrower view of the media impact than is perhaps justified. It is difficult to reject Richard Rose's conclusion that "In immediate electoral terms, the Conservative Party probably benefits from the tendency of the media to depress the quality of the nation's popular culture. . . . Parliamentary democracy as well as the Labour Party loses something from this."[17]

Many people believe that the introduction of commercial television symbolizes a change within the Conservative Party, which in turn reflects and expresses forces which are shaping British society. In simplest form this is described as the decline of aristocratic values and the substitution of commercial standards. It is not that trade and commerce are new to the Conservative Party, but rather that commercial standards and values have permeated more and more areas of British life as business regained its power and prestige after 1951.

One of the most forthright, not to say blunt, statements of this admittedly controversial thesis was provided by Mr. Peregrine Worsthorne, Conservative editorial writer for the London *Daily Telegraph*.[18] He believes that traditionally the Conservative Party was "an elaborate organization for keeping the right kind of people in power at all levels of the national life." The "right people" are those who "by birth, background, training and station are likely to be endowed with the rare knowledge of how to govern." Now it "might almost seem" that the Party had "become an elaborate organization for keeping the wrong men in power." This transformation is the achievement, Worsthorne believes, of "the hucksters, who were asked to attract the crowds, [but] have taken over the show. 'Give the people what they want' seems to have become not a means to an end, but an end in itself."

At the same time there has occurred what Ralph Samuels describes as "the upper-class colonization of business." The traditional ruling class, recruited from public schools as well as from retired officers and Cabinet officials, is "entering on the active commercial career." The result has been a decline of non-business class living, the disappearance of a different kind of life and the weakening of a competing standard of conduct and scale of values.[19] If continued, this development might justify Mr. Worsthorne's fear that the roots of the Conservative Party "are now so inextricably intertwined with the commercial complex producing the mass consumer goods, its voice so indistinguishable from the klaxon braying of commercialized culture, its electoral future so dependent on the mounting materialist momentum, that it cannot possibly stand apart, control, direct, modify or discipline; cannot, in short, fulfill its basic function of leadership in the very fields where leadership is most urgently required."

Throughout the debate on commercial television there is evident an open repudiation of those who conceived of the Conservative role as setting standards, or having concern for the quality of life. Mr. R. A. Butler could stress in 1946 the Conservative "belief that quality is as necessary as equality" and insist that "our particular contribution to the social philosophy of our time must be that we are guardians of tradition, that we bring all that is most inspiring in our past to serve the ever altering needs of our present."[20] By 1950 there were many in his Party eager to distinguish between "what the best people think and what the people think." The "new" Conservatives were prepared to be on the side of the people, so long as this meant electoral success and guaranteed advancement, privilege and power. In the guise of "democracy", of "setting the people free", of "giving the people what they want", there was a willingness to reject traditional Conservative doctrine. Cynical, pseudo-egalitarianism replaced an older commitment to the maintenance of national standards. Throughout the controversy it was apparent that the commercial advocates were contemptuous of efforts to uphold either cultural or intellectual standards;

the decisive consideration was that television was a great marketing device. They would certainly reject out of hand Worsthorne's insistence that "The most pressing task of government is to maintain the quality of the national life, the integrity of its institutions and the moral character of its people in face of the quite unprecedented impact of mass prosperity."

One is left with the impression that the Conservative leadership was something less than forthright in handling the television controversy. Britain was given commercial television against the advice of almost all the nominal leaders of society in education, religion and culture, as well as significant sections of the business community. At no time was the British electorate, or even the rank-and-file Conservative voter, given an opportunity of passing on the merits of the case. Lord Hailsham may have been extreme in characterizing the submission of the television bill to Parliament as "a shoddy and squalid constitutional error", but many believed there was justification for his criticism of the Government for its "deliberate concealment", in not presenting the issue for debate in the General Election. One cannot help but appreciate the extent to which the British Constitution is dependent on the character, sensibility and responsibility of those in positions of leadership.

REFERENCES

INTRODUCTION

[1] For a careful and stimulating evaluation of the impact on the BBC of Independent Television, see Burton Paulu, *British Broadcasting in Transition*, Minneapolis: University of Minnesota Press, 1961.

[2] For other accounts of British pressure politics see: S. E. Finer, *Anonymous Empire*: *A Study of the Lobby in Great Britain*. London: The Pall Mall Press Ltd., 1958; J. D. Stewart, *British Pressure Groups*: *Their Role in Relation to the House of Commons*, Oxford: The Clarendon Press, 1958; Harry Eckstein, *Pressure Group Politics*: *The Case of the British Medical Association*, Standford, California: Stanford University Press, 1960. Note especially Chapter I, "Theoretical Framework: The Determinants of Pressure Group Politics."

[3] A. A. Rogow, *The Labour Government and British Industry*, 1945-1951. Oxford: Basil Blackwell, 1955. (Especially Chapter VII.)

[4] Otto Kirchheimer, "The Waning of Opposition in Parliamentary Regimes," *Social Research*, Summer 1957, pp. 127-156.

CHAPTER I

[1] For the definitive history and evaluation of the BBC, see Burton Paulu, *British Broadcasting: Radio and Television in the United Kingdom*, Minneapolis: University of Minnesota Press, 1956. For detail on the origin of the monopoly position of the BBC,

see R. H. Coase, *British Broadcasting: A Study in Monopoly*, London: Longmans, Green & Co., 1950.

[2] The Broadcasting Committee, *Report*, Cmd. 1951, Paragraph 4, 6.

[3] Quoted in *Beveridge Report*, II, p. 39.

[4] Charters 1937-46; 1947-51; 1952-62. In July, 1960, another committee of inquiry was appointed under the chairmanship of Sir Harry Pilkington.

[5] Coase, *op. cit.*, p. 54.

[6] *Beveridge Report*, II, p. 364.

[7] Charles A. Siepmann, *Radio, Television and Society*, New York, 1950, pp. 129-130; see also Coase, *op. cit.*, Chapter 3; also P. P. Eckersley, *The Power Behind the Microphone*, London, 1941, p. 55. For Reith's comment on listener research see *Beveridge Report*, II, p. 364.

[8] For a fuller discussion of the relationship of the BBC to the Government, see Paulu, *British Broadcasting*, pp. 36-42, 92, et passim.

[9] *Beveridge Report*, II, p. 25.

[10] *Beveridge Report*, II, p. 364.

[11] *Beveridge Report*, I, p. 111.

[12] *Beveridge Report*, II, p. 544.

[13] Institute of Incorporated Practitioners in Advertising, *Broadcasting*, p. 7.

Chapter II

[1] House of Commons Debates, 418:693-94.

[2] H.C. Debs. 419:952-53.

[3] *Evening Citizen*, Glasgow, April 26, 1946.

[4] H.C. Debs. 421:1868-87.

[5] April 8, 1946; this point was also made most urgently by Conservative M.P. Butcher in the Commons debate on the White Paper, July 16, 1946, col. 1168.

[6] H.C. Debs. 424:171.

[7] H.C. Debs. 425:385-87.

[8] H.C. Debs. 331:645-46.

[9] H.C. Debs. 424:1321.

[10] H.L. Debs. 141-1173.

[11] H.L. Debs. 141:1175.

[12] H.L. Debs. 141:1175.

[13] H.L. Debs. 141:1184.

[14] H.L. Debs. 141:1217.

[15] H.L. Debs. 141:1216.

[16] *Broadcasting Policy* (Cmd. 6852) 1946.

[17] H.C. Debs. 425:1063-1179.

[18] "Lessons of the BBC Debate: Dangers Ahead," August 1, 1946.

[19] H.C. Debs. 389:32.

[20] July 3, 1946.

[21] "A Plan for Broadcasting," October 28, November 4, 11, 18, 1944.

[22] *Daily Mirror*, July 22, 1946.

[23] Letter, Michael Patmore, JWT, March 23, 1959.

[24] July 18, 1946.

[25] June 2, 1946.

[26] *Birmingham Mail*, July 3, 1946.

CHAPTER III

[1] May 21, 1949.

[2] October 13, 1949.

[3] *Report of the Broadcasting Committee* 1949, Cmd. 8116 and *Report of the Broadcasting Committee:* Appendix H: Memoranda Submitted to the Committee, Cmd. 8117.

[4] *The BBC from Within*, p. 34.

[5] *Beveridge Report*, I, p. 40.

[6] *Beveridge Report*, II, pp. 334, 335.

[7] *Beveridge Report*, I, p. 46.

[8] *Beveridge Report*, I, p. 46.

[9] *Beveridge Report*, I, p. 48.

[10] *Beveridge Report*, I, p. 43.

[11] *Beveridge Report*, I, p. 51.

[12] *Beveridge Report*, I, p. 165.

[13] *Beveridge Report*, I, pp. 47, 48.

[14] *Beveridge Report*, I, p. 168.

[15] *Beveridge Report*, I, p. 166.

16 See Lord Simon's discussion of this problem in *The BBC from Within*, pp. 60-74.

17 *Beveridge Report*, I, p. 100.

18 "Broadcasting: A Study of the case for and against commercial broadcasting under State Control in the United Kingdom," 1946; and Paper 112, *Beveridge Report*, II, pp. 542-546, September, 1949.

19 Letter, Michael Patmore, JWT, March 23, 1959.

20 IIPA Pamphlet, p. 27, 29.

21 IIPA Pamphlet, p. 16.

22 *Beveridge Report*, II, p. 542.

23 *Beveridge Report*, II, p. 545.

24 Interview, March 3, 1959.

25 *Beveridge Report*, I, p. 98.

26 *Beveridge Report*, I, p. 226.

27 *Beveridge Report*, I, p. 228.

28 *Beveridge Report*, I, p. 201.

29 *Beveridge Report*, I, p. 308.

30 *Beveridge Report*, I, p. 306.

31 *Beveridge Report*, I, p. 302.

32 *Beveridge Report*, I, p. 202.

33 *Beveridge Report*, I, p. 203.

34 *Beveridge Report*, I, p. 210.

35 *The BBC from Within*, p. 41.

36 *The BBC from Within*, p. 41.

37 Cmd. 8291, July, 1951.

38 H.C. Debs. 490:1423-1438.

39 H.C. Debs. 490:1453-1471.

40 H.C. Debs. 490:1479-1541.

41 H.L. Debs. 172:1213-1295.

CHAPTER IV

1 R. H. Coase, *British Broadcasting: A Study in Monopoly*, London, 1950. See also *Some Proposals for Constitutional Reform*, London: Eyre & Spottiswoode, Ltd., 1946, in which a group of Conservatives argue that a broadcasting monopoly is a "constitutional anomaly" and suggest, in addition to the BBC, networks under the British Arts Council and the British Council. (p. 17).

[2] "Advertising Angle," *World's Press News*, April 13, 1951.

[3] See p. 63, Chapter III.

[4] *News Chronicle*, October 10, 1953.

[5] *Sunday Express*, August 28, 1949.

[6] *Yorkshire Post*, September 12, 1952.

[7] Author of *Economics of Advertising* and *The Ethics of Advertising*.

[8] *Birmingham Mail*, April 25, 1947.

[9] *Edinburgh Evening Dispatch*, January 29, 1946.

[10] A point made by Mr. Selwyn Lloyd in his report to the Beveridge Committee; *Beveridge Report*, I, p. 306.

[11] Cmd. 8550, p. 3.

[12] *Memoirs*, pp. 327-328.

[13] "Memoirs of the Earl of Woolton," *The Sunday Times*, March 22, 1959.

[14] Interview, December 4, 1958.

[15] William D. Zabel, *The Transformation of the British Conservative Party from 1945 to 1951*. Princeton University Library, 1958. Unpublished Senior Thesis.

[16] Interview, December 4, 1958.

[17] "The Conservative Party and the Changing Class Structure," *The Political Quarterly*, April-June, 1953. pp. 139-147.

[18] *The Sunday Times*, March 29, 1959.

[19] *Memoirs*, p. 365.

[20] Interview with William D. Zabel, July 23, 1957, *op. cit.* pp. 87-88.

[21] Interview, December 4, 1958.

[22] Zabel, *op. cit.* p. 100.

[23] Interview, October 28, 1958.

[24] *Memoirs*, p. 377.

[25] *Memoirs*, p. 378; see also Churchill, *The Gathering Storm*, p. 468.

[26] Debate on the Ministry of Information (Mr. Brendan Bracken was Minister) H.C. Debs. 401:866.

[27] "Advertising Must Advertise," March 6, 1959.

[28] The Government ultimately gave in on the pension issue. See *News Chronicle*, March 3, 1954.

[29] Peter G. Richards, *Honourable Members: A study of the British Backbencher*, London, 1959. p. 92.

CHAPTER V

[1] H.L. Debs. 176:1293-1451.

[2] In support of their criticism of the Post Office, the Group cited R. H. Coase, *British Broadcasting: A Study in Monopoly.* See pp. 193-194.

[3] H.C. Debs. 502:213-342.

[4] March 3, 1952.

[5] *Beveridge Report,* II, p. 362.

[6] See pp. 40-41, Ch. II, for an account of Fraser's earlier position.

[7] H.C. Debs. 502:1952.

CHAPTER VI

[1] *News Chronicle,* June 24, 1953.

[2] *Anonymous Empire,* p. 49.

[3] London *Daily Recorder,* November 25, 1953.

[4] *Daily Express,* June 17, 1953.

[5] *The Economist,* July 30, 1949, p. 277.

[6] "Television: The Viewer and the Advertiser."

[7] See pp. 51-53, Chapter III.

[8] *World's Press News,* March 1, 1945.

[9] August 2, 1945.

[10] January 18, 1951.

[11] *Harrogate Advertiser,* October 3, 1953.

[12] *Advertisers' Weekly,* January 14, 1954.

[13] *The Times,* August 5, 1953.

[14] *Advertisers' Weekly,* October 29, 1953. For other examples, see letters of Mr. F. C. Hooper, Managing Director of Schweppes, Ltd., *The Times,* July 25, 1953. Hooper's position was supported by Mr. Richard Coit, Chairman of Paul E. Derrick Advertising Agency, ibid., July 30, 1953.

[15] Interview, November 17, 1958.

[16] *Manchester Guardian,* October 14, 1950.

[17] *Manchester Guardian,* September 21, 1949.

[18] *Manchester Guardian,* October 14, 1950.

[19] *The BBC from Within,* p. 71.

[20] *Manchester Guardian*, October 14, 1950.

[21] "Pendennis", September 18, 1955.

[22] Interview, November 17, 1958.

[23] Interview, March 25, 1959.

[24] Interview, January 21, 1959. He apparently began the campaign even earlier. See Tom Driberg, "Will This Kite Fly?" *New Statesman*, December 5, 1959.

[25] Interview, January 21, 1959.

[26] Letter to *The Times*, September 6, 1952.

[27] *The Times*, April 2, 1947.

[28] See Mr. Herbert Morrison's questions concerning Sir Robert Renwick's connection with the Government. H.C. Debs. 533:1142.

[29] *Daily Mail*, November 25, 1953.

[30] *Truth*, November 20, 1953.

[31] *New Commonwealth*, March 16, 1953.

[32] Memorandum to Beveridge Committee, written by Mr. Charles Orr-Ewing, *Beveridge Report*, II, p. 524.

[33] Speech by Vice-Admiral J. W. S. Darling of the Radio Industry Council to the Hampshire branch of the Radio & Television Retailers' Association, reported in the *Manchester Guardian*, October 15, 1949.

[34] *Financial Times*, November 5, 1949.

Chapter VII

[1] H.C. Debs. 513:1456-76.

[2] *Manchester Guardian*, July 22, 1953.

[3] *Daily Mirror*, July 23, 1953.

[4] *Urmston Telegraph*, October 22, 1953.

[5] October 1, 1953.

[6] *Liverpool Daily Post*, October 15, 1953.

[7] *Nottingham Evening Post*, September 24, 1953.

[8] Interview, December 4, 1958.

[9] Interview, March 18, 1959.

[10] Interview with Lord Bessborough, March 25, 1959.

[11] July 29, 1953.

[12] July 20, 1953.

[13] Interview, February 14, 1959.

[14] March 12, 1954.

[15] See also the *Borham Wood & Elstree Post*, Editorial, "Television," September 3, 1953.

[16] *Manchester Guardian*, November 4, 1953.

[17] October 30, 1953.

[18] August 20, 1953.

[19] Interview, March 2, 1959.

[20] Interview with Mr. Gordon McIvor, March 2, 1959.

[21] *Daily Mail*, October 29, 1953.

[22] *South Wales Echo & Express*, November 10, 1953.

[23] Ronald Simms, *Manchester Evening Chronicle*, October 16, 1953; Lord Foley, *Financial Times*, October 20, 1953.

[24] *Birmingham Gazette*, October 20, 1953.

[25] Membership leaflet, "The Facts About Competitive Television," p. 2, n.d.; Editorial, "Their Promise," *Bristol Evening Post*, September 25, 1953; Sir Robert Renwick, "Full Employment in the Radio Industry."

[26] *Liverpolitan & Merseyside Digest*, September 1, 1953.

[27] September 23, 1953.

[28] *Nottingham Guardian & Journal*, September 23, 1953.

[29] August 8, 1953.

[30] For similar notices see: *Music Teacher*, September, 1953; *World's Press News*, August 16, 1953; *Abra Cadabra* (magicians), August 8, 1953; *Art News & Review*, August 22, 1953.

[31] September 6, 1953.

[32] Interview, March 2, 1959.

[33] Interview, February 14, 1959.

Chapter VIII

[1] H.L. Debs. 176:1447, May 26, 1952.

[2] Guy Eden, in *Truth*, July 10, 1953.

[3] *Wiltshire Herald & Examiner*, September 4, 1953.

[4] August 9, 1953.

[5] *The Times*, October 9, 1953.

[6] *News of the World*, August 30, 1953.

[7] *The Times* and *Manchester Guardian*, October 2, 1953. The

Association pamphlet, "Commercial Television," March, 1954, sets forth the development of the Association's policy.

[8] Cmd. 9005.

[9] November 20, 1953.

[10] *World Press News*, November 20, 1953.

[11] *The Scotsman*, November 14, 1953. See also comments by Manchester advertising men in the *Manchester Evening News*, November 16, 1953.

[12] H.L. Debs. 184:743

[13] H.L. Debs. 184:741-743.

[14] P. A. Bromhead, *The House of Lords and Contemporary Politics, 1911-1957*, London: Routledge & Kegan Paul, 1958. p. 180.

[15] *News Chronicle*, November 20, 1953.

[16] See p. 89, Chap. IV.

[17] H.L. Debs. 184:552:561; 721:728.

[18] H.C. Debs. 522:141.

[19] Backbench Memorandum, November 18, 1953.

[20] Conservative Political Office to Members of Liaison Committee. Memorandum: Competitive TV—Time-Table. November 9, 1953.

[21] See statement by Selwyn Lloyd, H.C. Debs. 552:228, December 15, 1953.

[22] See the *Yorkshire Post* and *Leeds Mercury*, February 3, 1954. See also *The Times*, February 4, 1954.

[23] H.L. Debs. 188:188, June 30, 1954.

[24] Letter to *Birmingham Post*, March 25, 1954.

[25] Popular Television Association leaflet, "Memorandum on the Television Bill," n.d.

[26] H.C. Debs. 527:414, May 5, 1954.

[27] H.C. Debs. 529:329, June 22, 1954.

[28] H.C. Debs. 527:209, May 4, 1954.

[29] *Electrical & Radio Training* (London), April, 1954.

[30] *Daily Sketch*, March 15, 1954.

[31] *Nottingham Guardian Journal*, and *Liverpool Daily Post*, March 6, 1954.

[32] *World Press News*, March 12, 1954.

[33] March 11, 1954.

[34] Statement to *Advertisers' Weekly*, December 10, 1954.

[35] H.C. Debs. 527:416, May 5, 1954.

[36] *Birmingham Post,* Letter to the Editor, March 25, 1954.

[37] See above, p. 200.

[38] H.C. Debs. 529:330, June 22, 1954.

[39] Conservative Research Department Memorandum, "Television Bill: Principal Changes Made in the House of Lords," July 23, 1954.

CHAPTER IX

[1] S. E. Finer, *Anonymous Empire,* p. 99.

[2] R. T. McKenzie, *British Political Parties,* p. 279.

[3] Woolton, *op. cit.,* p. 356.

[4] Ibid., p. 348.

[5] See McKenzie, *op. cit.,* pp. 290-293.

[6] "Centraview: Journal of Central Ward Young Conservatives" No. 11 (September 1953), p. 2.

[7] H.C. Debs. 527:250-251 (May 4, 1953).

[8] McKenzie, *op. cit.,* p. 591.

[9] Quintin Hogg (Lord Hailsham), *The Case for Conservatism,* p. 111.

[10] "Television and Politics" manuscript written for *Truth,* March, 1953.

[11] *Memoirs,* p. 291.

[12] Richard Rose, "The Influence of Mass Media," *Crossbow,* Vol. 4, No. 13 (Autumn, 1960) p. 35.

[13] Conservative Political Centre, *The New Conservatism,* 1955, pp. 76-78; 136-138.

[14] S. E. Finer, *Anonymous Empire,* p. 92.

[15] "The Waning of Opposition in Parliamentary Regimes," *Social Research,* Summer, 1957.

[16] *Anonymous Empire,* p. 111.

[17] *Crossbow, op. cit.,* p. 35.

[18] "Affluent Society Engulfing Britain's Tories," *Washington* (D.C.) *Post,* January 24, 1960.

[19] E. P. Thompson (edit.) *Out of Apathy,* London: Stevens & Sons, 1960, pp. 36-42. See also Peter Shore, "In the room at the top," in Norman MacKenzie (edit.) *Conviction,* London: MacGibbon & Kee, 1958.

[20] *The New Conservatism, op. cit.,* p. 31.

INDEX